W9-CJT-990

Opportunity Screams

Opportunity Screams

Unlocking Hearts and Minds
in Today's Idea Economy

Tom Asacker

Paramount Market Publishing, Inc.

Paramount Market Publishing, Inc.
950 Danby Road, Suite 136
Ithaca, NY 14850
www.paramountbooks.com

Telephone: 607-275-8100; 888-787-8100
Facsimile: 607-275-8101

Publisher: James Madden
Editorial Director: Doris Walsh

Cataloging in Publication Data available
ISBN 13: 978-0-9819869-6-8 | ISBN 10: 0-9819869-6-X

For Ron

I say unto you: one must still have chaos in oneself
to be able to give birth to a dancing star.
I say unto you: you still have chaos in yourselves.
—Friedrich Nietzsche, *Thus Spoke Zarathustra:*
A Book for All and None

Carpé diem

Contents

At every corner, *Opportunity Screams.* It screams for more creativity, caring, and laughter. It screams for more meaningful and exciting organizations and experiences. And it's screaming for you to let go of your past and grab onto your future.

Our modern marketplace is awash in desperate attempts to attract people's attention. Unfortunately, attention is a flimsy concept. It's not built to last. We need a new way of thinking about how to connect with our audience; one that brings life to our ideas and brings our ideas to life.

We view the world through the lens of our own fears and desires, and this selective perception makes us focus on ourselves and our concerns. Success comes from opening our eyes, and our hearts, and connecting with others for their benefit and for ours.

Door Three: Belief

Page 69

Our relationship with our audience is based on nothing more than belief . . . and nothing less. Our belief in our ability to continuously surprise them, feed their hungers and make them feel proud of their association with us. And *their* heartfelt belief that we can.

Bring Your Idea to Life

Page 109

Now is not the time to "go along to get along." It's time to think very practically about how to uniquely add value to people's lives, and pursue those ideas with passion and daring. We are our ideas put into action. The Doors we open in the marketplace determine the destiny of those ideas.

Sign-Off

Page 117

About the Author

Page 118

Introduction

The world is all gates, all opportunities,
strings of tension waiting to be struck.
—Ralph Waldo Emerson

What's on your mind? What's bugging you? Whatever it is, for
your sake—and for those unwilling or unable to change—
come alive and do something about it! *Inspired action is the key
to unlocking the doors to opportunity, growth, and happiness.* The
inventor David Levy referred to it as the curse effect: "Whenever
I hear someone curse, it's a sign to invent something." Perhaps
that someone is you and that "cursing" is resonating between your
ears. Don't let those persistent screams irritate you and drain your
life and passion. Use them to fuel you and drive you forward.

Opportunity Doesn't Knock

Opportunity abounds, but you won't hear it knocking. Today
opportunity screams behind the closed doors of convention,
confusion, and fear. The future belongs to those unwilling to
accept the stifling status quo, to those who stay excited, puzzled,
and surprised. It belongs to those child-like people who are
constantly asking questions and wondering how things work, to
the geniuses.

That's right, geniuses!

How do you know when you're in the presence of genius? You witness a passionate, wide-eyed maniac who actually believes she can change things. I've been in the presence of genius. It's impossible to miss.

gen·ius [jeen-yuhs]: a person who strongly influences for good or ill the character, conduct, or destiny of a person, place, or thing.

Geniuses don't want to be products of their environment; they want their environment to be products of them. They are not observers and critics. They're dreamers and doers. They explore and create and, with their passion and daring, move us all forward.

A genius is a grade school teacher who stretches the "system" and inspires her students to greatness. She's a consultant who visualizes a radically new process and makes it come to life for the benefit of her clients and their risk-averse organizations.

A genius is an entrepreneur who feels the fear, but, like Sir Richard Branson, exclaims, "Screw it. Let's do it!" and pushes forward with a bold new idea. He's a leader who says, "What corporate doesn't know won't hurt them," and initiates a skunk works project that ends up changing the direction of the company.

Geniuses are *mis*fits. Like a pair of tight fitting pants, they're uncomfortable and they often make others uncomfortable.

Knowledge seldom leads to transformation. Rather, it is discomfort with the current reality that provokes change, and with it those unique experiences that inform and inspire us.

As the Dalai Lama put it, "Easy times are the enemy, they put us to sleep. Adversity is our friend, it wakes us up." Just ask the overweight, middle-aged person who has recently experienced a heart attack.

This Book is Dangerous

It won't give you a heart attack, but it may give you *restless mind syndrome*. If you sincerely consider its message and practice its principles it will transform the way you look at the world. It will become a mounting scream in your brain, pleading for you to take a chance and do interesting things. It will pester you, relentlessly, "What are you doing? Why are you doing it? Is it exciting? Are you proud of it? Is that the best that you can do?"

Will you become successful after reading this little book? That depends on how you define success. This is *not* a get rich quick, persuade others to your way of thinking type of handbook. It calls for less coaxing and more meaningful action. It demands that you get outside of your comfort zone and do something special, something *extra*ordinary.

After studying and speaking about the marketplace for the past 20 years, and teasing apart what works and what doesn't, I've discovered one universal truth: to flourish in a rapidly changing world you need to open your eyes, reframe your beliefs and usher in a constant stream of fresh insights.

Open your eyes. Ideas spring from awareness. Awareness will lift you from the shallows of mediocrity into the full and exciting sea of possibilities.

It's all Connected

I can still remember standing by my father's side at his little service station watching him break his back under his customers' cars—sweat pouring from his brow, black grease permanently embedded under his nails and into the cracks of his palms—only to see him wipe his hands as clean as possible, rest one gently on a concerned customer's shoulder, and calmly assure her that everything was okay. It was just a loose bolt or something. "And please," he'd say holding up his hands. "Put your wallet away. It was no big deal."

You know what? It was a big deal. It was the biggest of deals. And it has taken me far too long to appreciate the lesson he was trying to teach me: It's all connected. Transparent, honest, caring relationships bring meaning, happiness and growth to your business and to your life.

Integrity of Purpose

My dad loved cars, but not as an end; as a means. Cars were his way to connect with people. He was driven by their needs, not by his ego or the noise of the competitive environment. His garage ended up turning into a sort of sanctuary, where people from miles around would bring their problems, their favorite desserts, and their life stories. And my dad saw it as his purpose to take care of them all; to be their advocate and trusted advisor.

Whenever he thought he could use his connections and expertise to help save them time, money, or aggravation, he did it. He went deeper and deeper into his relationships, adding new products, sourcing new suppliers, doing anything that would add happiness to their lives.

Alas, my dad never did become "rich" by today's standards. But by focusing on what mattered most—incessantly and creatively adding significance and meaning to people's lives—he achieved more wealth than any person I've met in my thirty plus years in business.

Walt Disney had it figured out as well. His mantra was, "I don't make movies to make money. I make money to make movies." Do you see the difference? Disney's mission was to create first-rate entertainment and with it the happiness it brought to his audiences. He used money to continuously reinvent and realize that mission.

Most people do it the other way around; they create missions in order to make more money. What about you? What's your mission? Why do you make money?

If you've been putting off being passionate about your work in order to make a lot of money, now may be the time for you to make a change. The business of making money simply to make more money is quickly coming to an end.

The future is not in making a buck; it's in making connections and making a difference. It's about being interesting, creative, and vital. As Goethe wrote, "What is important in life is life, and not the result of life."

The Unifying Principle

A wise Rabbi once said, "If I am I because you are you. And you are you because I am I. Then I am not I and you are not you." It may sound like double-talk, but the teacher's message is a profoundly important one: we are not separate. We define

each other. We are fronts and backs of each other—producers/
consumers; government/citizens; actors/audience; manufacturers/
suppliers; consultants/clients; teachers/students; designers/users,
management/talent; you/me. In fact, you only know who you are
in terms of the other.

Unfortunately, we tell ourselves a very different story. We have
this notion that we're separate and that we can build our future
through a series of distinct, disconnected activities—clever
marketing to attract an audience; persuasive sales and follow-up
service to gain revenues and deal with problems; motivation to
keep the troops in line and moving.

The truth is everything and everyone is connected. In order to
describe who you are you must describe your behavior; what you
do. And to describe what you do, you must describe it—and all
activities associated with it—in *relationship* to your audience, to
your community.

What you are and how you evolve is what your community is
and how it evolves. It's integrative, interactive, and iterative. You,
therefore, are one, interdependent system of behavior. You are not
a separate thing.

Think of it this way: If you lean a bunch of sticks against each
other, they stand up because they support each other. Take
one away and the others become less stable, or they fall. Easy
to understand, but, like the childhood game "pick-up sticks,"
extremely complex and challenging to tease apart.

The hard work of value co-creation—viscerally understanding the
relationships between the sticks and strategically connecting them

to each other—is essential to unlocking the Doors to opportunity and achieving sustained success.

Stop and consider carefully whether your daily activities are propping up and supporting your audience, or adding even more noise and confusion to their busy lives. Are you strategically creating value, or are you pitching, broadcasting messages, and defending the status quo?

The key to a successful relationship lies out there, in the hopes, dreams, and real lives of your audience. Because what you do is not a separate, promotable thing. It's a *co-created* reality, experienced and enhanced with others.

Bringing Your Passion to Life

Have you ever heard the expression, "Do what you love and the money will follow?" There is a ring of truth to it, and it goes something like this: If you love it, you'll be open-eyed and curious about it. You'll study it, learn about it, and spend more time doing it. And all of this passion and attention (love) for what ever it is that you do will make you successful.

Passion is extremely important in business today, as well as in just about every other aspect of life. Certainly those who truly care and are genuinely excited about their professions will have an edge over others. But success in the marketplace has little to do with what *you* want.

Success is achieved by using your unique skills and enthusiasm to add value and happiness to the lives of *others*, by being a unique source of what turns *them* on.

The longing to improve life is the heart and soul of differentiation and success in today's marketplace. The challenge is to leverage your uniqueness and continuously innovate for their benefit over time. Or to put it another way: Do what they love, *with* what you love, and the money is sure to follow.

Real Wealth

Think about why you do what you do each day. Is it simply to grow your financial wealth, so that someday you can escape from people and relax with your grill and your pool, your gadgets and games? Or do you see each day for what it truly is; an opportunity to add a spark of meaning, caring and passion to life and to the lives of others?

Are you simply tolerating today, so that you can eventually arrive at a better tomorrow? Or do you realize that today *is* your life, and that it's the quality of your trip with others that really matters?

We all want peace of mind, this much is clear. And we believe that it comes from accumulating wealth, which it does. But it doesn't come from the illusory kind of wealth, the kind that fluctuates with economic conditions and life's circumstances. It comes from real wealth, the wealth of trusted friendships and caring relationships. The wealth of collaboration and creativity that flourishes and brings forth joy and comfort, in good times and in bad.

The Marketplace is Moving

Enlightened people are moving with the changing times. A passionate few have their shoulders pressed firmly against the demoralizing status quo and are pushing forward for the benefit of us all.

George Bernard Shaw had it right, "This is the true joy in life, the being used for a purpose recognized by yourself as a mighty one; the being thoroughly worn out before you are thrown on the scrap heap; the being a force of Nature instead of a feverish selfish little clod of ailments and grievances complaining that the world will not devote itself to making you happy."

The old obsession with wealth and fame—with winning and losing—is being replaced with purpose and contribution.

I'm afraid this book can't help you with integrity and purpose, I wish it could. But I can promise you this: If you are honest with yourself and with others, and you accept my premise that success comes from a dedication to working diligently to improve the lives of others, it will teach you how to bring your purpose and passion to life.

A Framework for Success

We all want to be excited. We all want to be winners. More importantly, we want to be uplifted by a worthy ideal. We want to be involved, treated with respect and recognized for our contributions. We want to make a difference. But here's the rub. The biggest issue in our businesses, work lives, and volunteer efforts is that we're disorganized.

We don't have a perceptual lens to bring the marketplace clearly into view. We have neither a unifying perspective that inspires us, nor a framework to guide our actions. Our notions of the way the world works, of what we're trying to accomplish, and of how to go about it are erroneous. We end up bouncing from one tactic to another, looking for shortcuts and tossing things against the wall to see if they'll stick.

We spend our days pickled in a world of parity, marinating in minutiae while our ideas and unbridled spirit shrivel up and die.

Grab yourself by the collar and yank yourself off of your comfortable, well-worn path and onto one brimming with excitement and buzzing with opportunity.

You are sitting on a rare opportunity, but you must be systematic in how you take advantage of it. It's how you frame the situation that will dictate your outcome.

A New Mindset

Opportunity Screams is not an improved set of tactics; it's a new way of thinking designed to open your eyes to new possibilities. In the chapters that follow, you will be introduced to a lens for viewing and seizing opportunity that most people are unaware of.

It is not a formula. Formulas are rules for followers designed to produce sameness. They limit and obscure opportunities to create something unique.

There are no rules in this book, or in the marketplace of ideas. But there are patterns that you need to pay attention to. *Opportunity Screams* will reveal those patterns and present a framework that will provide clarity, stretch your mind and empower you to bring your purpose and passion to life. It will help you put together ideas and information in unique and powerful combinations that nobody else has done before.

The goal of this book is *not* to defend the framework against all criticism. Rather it's to present a road map and various routes to inspire and energize you, to help unleash the power of ideas and transform them into meaningful actions. It is not a sure-fire, fill-in-the-blanks algorithm. It's a way of seeing and evaluating ideas that will increase your probability of a successful outcome and get you there more quickly.

Once you are in the habit of using it, it will help you deconstruct and demystify the diverse patterns of the ever-shifting marketplace kaleidoscope, as well as reveal the rationale for various successes and failures.

More importantly, the framework will inspire confidence and risk-taking. It will drive you to understand the design of your strategy and embrace *your* uniqueness—that powerful emotional idea that distinguishes you and will motivate others.

The essence of the framework is based on how people in a culturally mature, choice-driven marketplace perceive the world, and how they make decisions and recommendations. The *spirit* of this little book, however, lies in the great photographer Cecil Beaton's impassioned plea:

"Be daring, be different, be impractical, be anything that will assert integrity of purpose and imaginative vision against the play-it-safers, the creatures of the commonplace, the slaves of the ordinary."

Everyone has an agenda and an opinion. Everyone has their reasons why this or that won't work. And the result of all of this griping and second-guessing is that nothing happens.

For me, trying something new and making things happen is what life is all about. Action is character. You are what you do.

I Never Met a Metaphor I Didn't Like

In our current world of information overload, good metaphors and analogies can provide clarity and guidance during challenging situations. They create new ways of seeing, which lead to new ways of being. One mental image is the concept of locked doors and keys.

In the framework that follows, the locked Doors represent the mental states that must be motivated in others to attract their attention, sustain their interest, and inspire them to act.

The Locks represent *your* limiting beliefs—the mental *barriers* that prevent you from being original and connecting in interesting and meaningful ways.

The Keys are, literally, the key. They'll refresh your tired eyes, reframe your reality and help you affect others. The Keys will unlock the Doors to opportunity.

Each Key has a unique shape, or Design, which is essential to unlocking a particular Door. Use the Keys and embrace the spirit of their specific Designs, and you will increase your chances of marketplace success. Ignore them and it will slow you down, cost you more time and money than necessary, and, most likely, frustrate the living hell out of you.

Door One: Engagement

How do we create awareness *and* engage very busy people? Unlocking the first Door—the Door to Engagement—is about being captivating, so that the people who can benefit from what you do become enchanted and compelled to investigate further.

If you've invested in something and are passionate about it, then you should at the very least be able to get people's attention and interest. I can assure you, however, that it is not as simple as it may seem.

The brain is a lazy piece of meat that conserves energy by taking the safe path, following routines and making predictions about the future based on past experiences. It sees what it wants to see and does what it *feels* like doing, regardless of what you think it should. And it's getting lazier and more myopic as today's culture of distraction adapts to searching, clicking, scanning, and media snacking.

We live in a highly filtered, short message world buzzing with people who are anxious about their livelihood; confused and tired of conflicting information; and bedazzled by technology and media. To be discovered by these overwhelmed brains and connect with them in a meaningful way, you must go beyond the ordinary and engage them with an unconventional and carefully considered approach.

Door Two: Interest

Once you engage people, you must strategically make use of that opportunity to signal meaning and value. By doing so, you'll motivate them to dig deeper and *maintain* their interest.

Unlocking the Door to Interest is about drawing *curious people* towards you by creating something valuable and memorable. It must be something that connects deeply with their desires and sense of self; something that will, ultimately, move them to action.

Unlocking the first Door, and engaging people with a unique approach, may temporarily shine a light on your creativity and your offering. Opening the second Door and sustaining their interest, however, is about releasing the grip of your ego and desires, and turning that light back around on *them*.

Door Three: Belief

Belief is the confident expectation of something or someone. Nothing happens without belief. So what engenders belief in an era of mistrust and cynicism?

Unlocking the Door to Belief is about being *real*, so that *interested people* become customers — or fans, donors, users, voters, patients, clients, followers, et al.

You create belief by demonstrating unique value, not by talking about it. You create belief by being human and passionate in your approach to the world. You create belief by making what you do vivid and tangible, and by helping your audience see your idea brought to life in *their* world for the benefit of people like them.

That's it. Your audience is engaged, they're interested, and most importantly, they believe. They believe in your imaginative vision. They believe in your integrity of purpose. They believe in the special meaning and value you'll add to their lives, and to the lives of people like them. They believe in you and your idea.

But will your audience look forward to seeing you? Will they proffer advice to help you improve what you do and keep you ahead of the pack? Will they refer their family and friends? Will they continue to believe?

They will if you continue to unlock their Doors with emotion, passion and daring creativity, and keep them engaged and interested. Doing so will complete the pulsating and ever-expanding circle called relationship, and reinforce your audience's decision to believe in you and make you a part of their lives.

There Are No Shortcuts

There are only three Doors, but there are no shortcuts. You must put in the time and effort to unlock each one to have any chance of perpetual success; success that builds upon itself. You'll be happy to know, however, that no special expertise is required. And distinctions like age, gender and profession are irrelevant. You *just* have to be a genius and have the creativity and guts to move forward, to continuously surprise, engage and inspire people with new and valuable ideas.

Given the rapidly changing times we live in today, the opportunity to touch people's lives in interesting and meaningful ways is virtually limitless. What stops most people and organizations is a lack of purpose, creative idleness, and plain, old-fashioned fear. They're driven by numbers and angst, and have fallen morally and creatively asleep.

Don't let those things happen to you. Wake up and seize this opportunity to experience and grow, while others snuggle deeper into their comfy routines. Confront what's in front of you with a clear and flexible mind. Be courageous *and* considered. Spirited *and* sensible. Go confidently in the direction of your beliefs and dreams. You'll be happily surprised by what you discover.

At the end of the short chapter about each Door is a list of questions to reflect upon. Within those questions are highlighted keywords. Type a highlighted word into the search box at *www. opportunityscreams.com*, and it will launch a short video on the topic at hand.

Rather than writing a *thick* book, I thought you'd prefer a thin one with the option to dive into more engaging and valuable content when the opportunity best suits you and your team.

Ben Franklin once advised, "Either write something worth reading or do something worth writing about." I say, "Screw it. Do both!"

On to Door One!

DOOR ONE
Engagement

When you can do the common things of life in an uncommon
way, you will command the attention of the world.
—George Washington Carver

Commanding the *attention* of the world may have been a worthy
accomplishment in Carver's time. Today, everyone is doing it. It's
as effortless as announcing that your son has been whisked into
the sky by a giant UFO-like helium balloon.

Attention is a Flimsy Concept

Attention is the end game played by reality TV wannabes,
"famous for being famous" media personalities, and other
self-interested or low-involvement ideas. And indeed, it may be
enough to drive their agendas since, like peanuts and Paris Hilton,
they're chosen primarily *because* of their ubiquity and popularity.

But it's not wise to rely on mere awareness, especially not in
today's message saturated and highly discriminating marketplace.
Instead, you want your idea to stand out and capture people's
engagement.

"But," you may be thinking. "People were engaged with Balloon
Boy's story? After all, they did spread it around."

It was certainly a sticky story. In fact, it was so sticky that people got stuck on the *story* and never made a connection to their *lives*. The story wasn't built to last. It didn't *deeply* engage anyone, because it didn't really *matter* to anyone.

Opportunity Screams is about enduring engagement. It's about using attention as a lever to open the next two Doors—the Doors to Interest and Belief—and create lasting connections, not casual ones.

It's about understanding culture, and feeding people's dreams and desires. It's about turning people on to your idea and bringing it to life by connecting it emotionally and meaningfully to their lives. It's about turning heads *and* changing minds.

It's a Dance

You don't want people to stick to the dance floor, to simply know your name and sing your song. You want them to glide through a frictionless, evolving process that excites their sensibilities and gently unlocks their minds and hearts for what you do and have to offer. *Opportunity Screams* is about relentlessly innovating for your audience's benefit, and for yours.

Unlocking this first Door is about answering one simple and essential question: *How do we engage people so they'll dig deeper into who we are and what we have to offer?*

Engagement is about getting people lost in the experience, in the expectation of what will happen next. It's about being fascinating in a way that draws people closer to you, because they may desire your idea. It's about unexpected relevance that communicates visually and emotionally. Above all else, it's about creativity and courage.

THE LOCK

Here is the Lock, your brain jam: You're afraid to change your pattern and do something truly fascinating. You don't want to call attention to yourself for fear of trivializing what you do or appearing brash or desperate.

You're mature and realistic. You dismiss being captivating as insincere, childish or showy.

Or maybe the economic environment has caused you to become risk-averse and penny-wise. You're unwilling to invest in the new—the hard work, creative talent and ideas required to bring what you do to life—without first "knowing" what that future may bring.

Stop trying to protect yourself from an unknowable future by doing more of the same. It will only bring you more of the same. Instead, be a connected and passionate catalyst of an unfolding story; one that you help script and bring to life.

THE KEY

Here's the Key: Come alive and be captivating.

When *Fortune* Magazine's CEO of the decade, Steve Jobs, steps onto a stage, the audience sits on the edge of their seats with eager anticipation. Not for his rhetorical mastery, but rather for this master of suspense's imaginative vision.

They're mesmerized by "insanely great" music players with eye-catching white headphones; laptops so thin they fit in manila envelopes; mobile phones *without* keypads; a game changing multimedia tablet; and elegant ecosystems of music, movies, books and apps.

I know you're probably sick of hearing it, but Steve Jobs and Apple get it. They understand that the ability to "think different" comes from the will and courage to act different.

Apple continues to violate people's mounting expectations, including stock analysts, with each new idea—irresistible, intuitive ideas that are beautiful and work beautifully. And this perpetual surprise keeps their audience's minds and hearts engaged and wondering, "What's next? When?"

The writer and scholar Joseph Campbell said, "I don't believe people are looking for the meaning of life as much as they are looking for the experience of being alive." Being captivating is about creating that feeling with and for others . . . over and over again.

It's about being where people live—online or off, in reality or in their heads—and adding some color and enjoyment to their lives. It's about intriguing them, so they'll pause from their chaotic and networked existence and dig deeper for more information, more ideas, and more meaning.

Theatre and Substance

There's a theatre part to your work and there's a substance part. Like the front and back of a coin, theatre and substance are inseparable components of a successful idea.

Theatre is about insights and originality. It's about flexibility, and bursts of creativity and intensity. It's unexpected, like an admiring comment that makes you smile or an arresting design that grows your eyes wide.

Substance is about mastery, planning and consistency. It's disciplined and process-oriented. It's expected, like someone getting you to your destination on-time or a public restroom that's spotless and shines.

The Power Lies in the Combination

Theatre *and* substance. Originality *and* mastery. Hearts *and* minds.

It's like working out. Structure and repetition is what brings results, but *only* if you introduce change and bursts of intensity to shock and confuse the muscles.

Muscles love routine. Routine *feels* good. Your brain is a muscle.

Change without discipline is foolhardy and dangerous. And mastery without originality and spontaneity becomes monotonous. And in today's marketplace, deadly.

The Door to Engagement screams for theatre; originality attracts and inspires. However, you're not simply trying to shock people or get a laugh. You're also not trying to be enticingly vague so that you can hook 'em and reel 'em in with your perfectly polished pitch. That's a tired and instrumental approach, and people can see right through it.

You want to bring what you do to life in a meaningful and compelling way and create excited anticipation for something more;

something people believe will provide answers, and bring happiness to their lives.

You want them to be turned on by your idea and compelled to dig deeper, beyond the surface to the powerful passionate core.

This isn't about you and your creativity. It's about something bigger. It's about life and your idea for improving life.

Puzzle Them

Through his passion for boxing and his embodiment of theatre, Muhammad Ali brought the idea of liberation through self-validation to life for millions. And that's what truly made him "The Greatest." He once remarked, "People like to be puzzled. So I puzzle them."

People want to be fascinated and drawn in by your idea. It breaks *their* monotony, inspires them, and helps them direct their limited time and attention. It also gives them something interesting to experience and share with others.

If you believe deeply in the value of what you do, if you truly feel that you can help improve people's lives (even a few people), then get your courage up and do something fascinating. You're robbing your fellow human beings if you don't do everything you can to yank them off of *their* well-worn paths and move them towards your idea.

You're also short-changing your life. You have a responsibility to be a steward of the unique gifts you were given. So do it! That's when the real excitement and real learning begins. Just make sure that your diversion is a fascinating and desirable one. One that adds value to their lives; like Ali's Thrilla in Manila, an iPhone, or a piano stairway.

Stairway to Engagement

When you're making your way through an airport or subway station, do you typically take the stairs or ride the escalator? Most people choose the latter, less healthy option, because riding the escalator is, frankly, more enjoyable. That changed for a few days in August 2009 in Stockholm when Volkswagen Sweden anonymously converted the stairway in a subway station into a giant, working piano keyboard.

The idea was part of an initiative called thefuntheory.com, which, as their website explains, is "dedicated to the thought that something as simple as fun is the easiest way to change people's behaviour for the better."

As of this writing, that particular example of imaginative vision has had more than 12 million views on YouTube.

The Connection is what Counts

That's a lot of eyeballs, but eyeballs and memories are fleeting —especially in an age overflowing with well-funded attempts to attract people's attention. To transcend all of that creative noise, you need a meaningful connection to a central idea—an idea that moves people to take action.

It's the connection, and the subsequent behavior, that creates long-term engagement and advances an idea.

Certainly, Volkswagen didn't create intrigue and fun *simply* to entertain people. Thefuntheory.com is but one creative attempt by VW to help its audience make a connection between life improvement and VW's environmentally friendly cars.

Are your creative efforts making a connection? Or are they simply capturing attention and getting a laugh?

The Spirit Behind the Actions

A piano stairway is a somewhat pricey example of creating something captivating that draws people in for further inquiry or engagement. But being captivating has little to do with your financial investment. It has everything to do with creativity and courage.

It's about discovering opportunities to make life better for people. It's about taking the time and making the effort to engage their attention and interest in a fresh way, and connecting it to a meaningful idea—*your* meaningful idea.

It's no longer enough to simply get and keep people's attention. Balloon Boy had people's attention, and so do a plethora of heavily promoted products and businesses that people are no doubt aware of, yet have never considered making a part of their lives.

Unlocking the Door to Engagement is about going deep and uncovering hidden insights—those silent screams that long to be heard and recognized—and tapping into those feelings to craft products, programs, and activities that enrich people's lives.

An executive at a well-known footwear company once muttered

to me, "I don't need more data. I've got millions of dollars worth of information piled up in the next room. What I need to know is what to *do* with it all."

He needs insights. So do you. Insights lead to ideas. And ideas inspire action.

THE DESIGN

Whether it's an ad, a package, a résumé, a new product, a speech, or a piano staircase, the Design of the Key that unlocks the stubborn Door to Engagement is always the same. A pattern that opens hearts and minds no matter who we are, where we live, or what we believe in.

First, be unexpected. Being unexpected is the attention-getter. Break through the complacency of your audience's typical experience by doing or saying something novel, something unanticipated.

Next, communicate in an expressive way. Communicating in an expressive way is the attention-sustainer. Focus on appealing to people's guts with your look and feel. You're trying to charm and inspire, rather than impress and convince.

Finally, be evocative. Don't be different for the sake of being different. Weave in a cue to your future significance in their lives. Give them a reason to take further action. To paraphrase Jerry Mcguire, "Show them the value!" Being evocative is the attention-mover.

People are extremely time-starved and skeptical. They're quickly trying to discern value as they rapidly move through today's supersaturated, confusing and rapidly changing marketplace. This new reality demands that you appeal *first* to their feeling system, and then to their thinking system.

And you start by being unexpected.

UNEXPECTED

When was the last time you were intrigued and pleasantly surprised? Think about it, I'll wait.

The fact that it's taking you some time to remember reveals something critically important: It's scarce. And scarcity is what drives value in any marketplace.

As the author Gilles Deleuze wrote, "We do not lack communication. On the contrary, we have too much of it. We lack creation. We lack resistance to the present."

Resist the present. Quit self-promoting and pushing information. Stop trying to impress and persuade. As the management guru and "wizard of wow!" Tom Peters makes clear, "Communication is everyone's panacea for everything."

Kick the habit. Create something unexpected and provocative that surprises people and touches their emotions. Arouse their attention by being out of the ordinary—*un*usual—and tease them into your details by charming them and having some fun.

Unexpected is more than different. It's a difference that stops people in their tracks.

Unexpected is a piano staircase.

It's also a hand-written letter rising out of a sea of bulk mail. Free shipping on all orders, including returns.

It's an out-of-the-blue call from a business owner to thank you for your business.

Unexpected is a pop-up retail store. It's a cover letter that talks passionately about the recipient, instead of the sender. It's a freshly baked banana bread delivered to your hotel room when you check-in.

Unexpected is someone speaking the unvarnished truth in a passionate, yet caring way. It's a person on fire with a mission to improve people's lives. It's a touching or hilarious, and true-to-life, video.

Unexpected *was* a yellow rubber wristband or white headphones on a stranger sitting next to you (critical components of the success of the LiveStrong and iPod ideas).

Unexpected Means Just That

It is not what we expect in our mailbox, on someone's wrist, in our path, on a billboard, or to spring from the mouths of most people. If it is, we simply ignore it. Or compare it. Or forget about it.

Be brave, step out of the darkness of similarity and do something bright, inspiring and meaningful. Be bold. Be unexpected. Empathize and engage people when they're desperate for a diversion, for a surprise.

Just make sure to quickly communicate the *right* message in an expressive, relationship-building way.

EXPRESSIVE

Prior to President Obama's election, U.S. Senator Harry Reid told two journalists that Obama, as a black candidate, could be successful due, in part, to his "light-skinned" appearance and speaking patterns "with no Negro dialect, unless he wanted to have one."

Was Reid's statement accurate? Perhaps. So what?

The content of his message—the words—were intended to communicate in a rational, *informative* manner; to transfer *understanding*.

Informative is simple. Informative is what you say.

The *expressive* nature of his communication, however, conveyed a more nuanced *meaning*. It transferred *presumed* cultural intelligence, racial sensitivity and *feelings*.

Expressive communication is hard. It's about what they hear *after* you've finished saying what you have to say.

Everything Communicates

You know *what* you want to say, but do you know *how* to say it? It's the how—the transfer of *presumed* intent, competence and feelings—that's key.

People make their own meaning based on what they see and experience—what they *feel*—not on what you say. And that *feeling* is a feeling of knowing—knowing who you are, what you're about, and, especially, what you're after.

How people respond to what you say has more to do with *why* they think you said it, than with *what* was literally said.

Expressive communication communicates the *why*. It sends a message that tells people how passionate you are and how dedicated you are to your idea. And that expresses how passionate*ly* you'll strive to be a perfectionist and a protagonist for them.

Reportedly, Steve Jobs refuses to display *No-Smoking* signs in his U.K. Apple stores, even though they are required by law. He'd rather pay the hefty daily fine, than corrupt the exquisite Apple experience.

Geniuses are unreasonable about what they stand for and how they bring their ideas to life. Be unreasonable.

The More You Say, the Less People Hear

You do *not* communicate. You become *part of* communication. And believe it or not, the best message is one that conveys clear and coherent meaning, yet people typically have no idea that they've received it. It communicates purpose and meaning at a subconscious level, while favorably affecting feelings and behavior.

Most ads, websites, packages, direct mail pieces, billboards, emails, and presentations communicate in a dispassionate and confusing way, sending mixed and unintended messages. And, like Senator Reid, the very clever creators are completely unaware of it.

Are you aware? Do you understand and embrace the fact that the meaning of your message is the response it elicits? That when you communicate a message—whether you do so face-to-face, to a group, over the telephone, on the Internet, over the airwaves, or in writing—the message means what the receiver of the message *thinks* it means?

Don't even consider the figment defense of *mis*perception. There's no such thing. There's only perception. Perception is all there is.

And perception is your job.

Can you creatively engage people so they'll create *your* meaning for themselves, a meaning that's important to them? Can you quickly get your message across without saying anything, without literal verbal language, supporting information and comparative data? Can you express your uniqueness without being overt or obvious?

It's tough. But that's the goal with this Door.

It's about communicating in a culturally and contextually relevant way, a way that transfers a message of empathy and distinctive value without the recipient being *consciously* aware of it.

Expressive communication is an empathetic and caring physician taking the time to learn about you and your life. It's the aesthetically pleasing, yet simple design and user interface of a website or product.

Expressive communication is a heartfelt, hand-written letter. It's the solid sound of a luxury car door closing. It's the witty saying on a church billboard. It's a distinctive Tiffany blue box tied up with a signature white ribbon.

Expressive communication is a homeless person selling magazines to benefit the destitute, standing next to a sign that reads, "Free Delivery within 10 Feet."

Informative communication is a sign that reads, "Open 7 days a week." Expressive is, "Happiness Available 7 Days a Week."

Expressive is *New Pig*, a leading industrial maintenance company, referring to their catalog as a "Pigalog" and their customers as "partners in grime."

But . . . expressive is also arms folded across a tense chest. Pop up ads. A phone call at dinner time. An email that looks like an infomercial. A computerized voice mail system with no obvious way to opt out and speak with a human being.

Expressive communication done well is a hauntingly beautiful product shot displayed on super high-quality paper. It's the brilliantly strategic execution of an engaging advertisement. It's the passionate conviction in the voice of a company representative. It's the company you keep.

Expressive communication is poetry. Informative communication is an instruction manual.

Informative is them hearing *your* words. Expressive is you engaging the voice in *their* heads.

EVOCATIVE

I typically take the same route home from my office each evening. You probably do, too. Researchers have discovered that close to fifty percent of what we do each day is done at the same time *and* in the same place. We are truly creatures of habit.

I also have a particularly dicey tendency of exceeding the posted speed limit. But only on side roads, since cruise control saves me on the highway.

One day last October, something else saved me on a winding country road that leads to my home. It also saved a family on an early evening stroll.

It was dusk. The New England trees, which ten minutes earlier were exploding with color, were mere shadows against a darkening sky. I was neck deep in the process of writing this book, spinning thoughts and chewing on metaphors as I raced around the final turn towards my house.

Suddenly, my brain shot from miles away to fully focused. You've probably seen those large speed indicator display signs; the ones that are left on the side of the road to flash your vehicle's MPH as you approach.

I'd seen them before, but never on that stretch of road. In fact, I wasn't really sure what it was at first, so my eyes naturally shot over to the flashing display.

And then my mind came along for the ride: *45 mph . . . 40 . . . 36 . . . 30! Nailed it! And look?! I made a smiley face appear on the display. Cool.*

I continued to be engaged with my speedometer until I arrived home, which, thankfully, helped me avoid a potentially tragic accident with a family all dressed in black and wandering aimlessly into the road.

Because of my mindset at that time, the speed sign appeared as a *near* perfect example of using the correct Design to unlock the Door to Engagement.

It was *unexpected*. It surprised me. I didn't expect to see it on that road and at that time of day. Also, the message was conveyed where and when I was most receptive to it. I didn't have to change myself or my routine to experience it. It was designed to fit into my life.

It also communicated in an *expressive* fashion. The interactive nature of the changing display made it *feel* like a game, which caused me to listen to my internal voice and play along. The sign put me in control of my thoughts, and in control of it.

In addition, the sign conveyed a sense of empathy and relationship. Its smiley face turned a perfectly rational, yet potentially threatening and authoritative message— *You! Slow down*—into a friendly, and more collaborative one— *Look what we did? Cool.*

But here's where the Door to Engagement remained locked: There was nothing truly *evocative* about the sign. The experience was relevant and valuable in and of itself, and it did, indeed, motivate my short-term behavior. But no attempt was made to engage me in a deeper way by signaling further meaning or value.

It was a one-off stimulus. There was no way for me to learn more or participate and add even more significance to my life and to the lives of my family and friends.

So, did the sign do its job? Yes and no. Yes, it had an effect on my head, my immediate thinking and behavior. But—and this is the problem with most short-term, attention-grabbing techniques—it had no affect on my gut. It didn't help me internalize a message of value. It didn't stimulate desire.

It was like most tweets, sales promotions or even sales encounters.

Once someone removes the stimulus—or introduces a more entertaining or persuasive one—the behavior goes with it.

The sign got only two-thirds of the Design right. It missed the final notch on the Key to the Door to Engagement; it wasn't *evocative*.

Different day. Different road. Better metaphor.

I was still driving too fast (another side road). And again my attention was grabbed and engaged by something unusual on the side of the road. But this time I was compelled to dig deeper, both figuratively and literally.

I was bewildered, this time, by a crowd of people gathered around a mind-trippy, upside-down-looking truck. I slowed down and removed my sunglasses to get a clearer view, and discovered a weird, multi-colored promotional vehicle.

Everyone looked like they were enjoying themselves, so I pulled over to check it out. I strolled up to the truck and discovered ice cream brand Ben & Jerry's and its new *Flipped Out! Sundaes*; a single-serve sundae in a cup designed to be tipped upside down to enjoy.

Without being consciously aware of what was happening, my Door to Engagement was unlocked and kicked open by an unexpected, highly expressive *and* evocative piece of corporate creativity. The next thing you know, I'm smiling, licking a spoon and mentally adding the *Flipped Out! Sundae* idea to my sub-conscious shopping cart.

A Cue to Value

Evocative does more than evoke a feeling or mood. It conjures up meaning and value. It answers the question we all experience when presented with something novel, "So what?"

Evocative is a message hinting at "what's in it for me."

The price of a bottle of wine is evocative. It conveys value. So does the cold-activated label on a can of Coors beer.

A dark silhouette on an arty billboard, rocking out while wearing white headphones and clutching a tiny iPod is both expressive and evocative. Nike's swoosh on a star athlete is evocative.

Blurbs on the back of a book's dust jacket are evocative. So is BMW saying that the Mini Cooper's unique steering system produces a "go-kart-like ride."

A stirring ninety-second trailer for a documentary movie is evocative. So is a five-star rating from someone you respect.

Evocative sends a signal of value that turns people on to your idea. Signals matter. Signals create expectations, which motivate choice *and* influence actual experiences.

What signals are you sending?

DOOR ONE SUMMARY

The Door to Engagement is rusted shut. You know this, intuitively. You're aware that people have far too many choices to deal with; too much information to process, most of which is conflicting; and, they simply don't trust information from organizations or the people who run them.

But you persist. You knock, knock, knock with uninspiring messages and meaningless behavior.

It's been said that the definition of insanity is doing the same things over and over and expecting different results. It's also insane, especially is a rapidly changing world, to do the same things over and over while expecting the same results (or even comparable ones).

Don't be insane. Change.

But don't change for the sake of change. Don't try to *create* opportunity by being novel. *Discover* opportunity and create value with bold, novel ideas.

You can tweet and follow and blog and upload videos and dance in the streets until your fingertips bleed and your shoes fall apart and you'll never truly engage people. Not until you've created something original and compelling. Something that turns you on and draws them in. Something that you've mastered and they desire. Something you *and* your audience care deeply about.

Perhaps that something is content; heaven knows the world needs more great writing, music, photography, and filmmaking. Music lifts our souls. We're transformed by a compelling photograph and inspired by a rousing speech. Movies and theatre help mold our sentiments. Humor keeps us sane.

Whatever *it* happens to be, go for the gut. Make it bold. Be inventive. Charm people. Take a stand and make it significant . . . to them.

And then move beyond engagement and on to the Door to Interest.

QUESTIONS TO ASK YOURSELF ABOUT
THE DOOR TO ENGAGEMENT

Is *it* captivating? Is *it* unexpected? Is *it* completely different than what they've come to expect from *it*?

Have we made it easy for them to engage with *it*? Is *it* designed to fit their lives and their behavioral predispositions?

Does *it* stir their emotions and engage their conscious attention? Have they internalized *it*?

Is *it* expressive? Does *it* speak our intentions and distinctiveness on *its* own, without literal, verbal language?

Is *it* evocative? Does *it* create an expectation of value? Does the uniqueness of what we do, and offer, come alive through *it*?

Does *it* drive follow up behavior; will folks seek out more information, talk to others, request a sample, etc.?

Does *it* move them forward? Will *it* bring them back?

Great!

On to Door Two.

DOOR TWO

Interest

Just because I don't care, doesn't mean I don't understand.

—Homer Simpson

"Bigger than the internet? As important as the PC? Mystery surrounds renowned inventor's latest 'technological wonder'."

That headline was penned close to a decade ago by Charles Arthur, then Technology Editor for *The Independent,* to express how people like Jeff Bezos, Steve Jobs, and other visionaries felt about "Ginger," the two-wheeled, self-balancing electric scooter invented by Dean Kamen. Arthur modified the punctuation of the VIP's expressed sentiments towards "IT" (another code name for Kamen's idea), changing from exclamation points to question marks. It was a prophetic decision.

Ginger, "IT," the Segway HT (human transporter) was billed as an earthshaking innovation. And indeed, it was an unexpected wonder that communicated its uniqueness in an absolutely unexpected and evocative manner.

It was unveiled on ABC's *Good Morning America* to millions and, through extensive media coverage, captivated the masses. Even the President of the time, George W. Bush, was shown riding a Segway. And falling off.

So what happened?

Not much. Even though the media and seers trumpeted the idea, and its inventor predicted that it "will be to the car what the car was to the horse and buggy," sales of the Segway have been lackluster. In fact, *Time Magazine* listed it as one of the ten biggest tech failures of the last decade.

Why? Because despite being beautifully designed, well-funded and highly-publicized, it's not what an idea *is* that matters in today's marketplace. It's what the idea *does*. And as an idea, the Segway simply didn't do anything for the masses. It wasn't relevant to most people's lives. It wasn't desirable.

The Lie of the Mind

One of the most pernicious myths in the marketplace of ideas is that the Door to Interest is opened with media exposure and salesmanship. Dean Kamen believed it. Most politicians rely on it. And Google makes billions appealing to it.

Why does it persist? Because there are a lot of people whose imagined futures, self-worth, and livelihoods are tied up in that myth. They suffer from what Nassim Taleb, author of the influential book *The Black Swan,* calls the "narrative fallacy," the notion that people sometimes explain events by cooking up stories—by reverse engineering an explanation.

The cooked-up story about this Door is that people become interested in something, in an idea, because they're repeatedly exposed to it or are otherwise *conditioned* or *convinced* to take interest. And then their interest *in* the idea eventually leads to desire *for* the idea.

The fact is very much the opposite. As author and neurologist Robert A. Burton points out, "In order to pursue a new thought, we must *feel* the thought is worth pursuing *before* we have any supporting evidence or justification." In other words, desire stimulates interest.

Despite the increasing flood of advertising dollars and the explosion of media consumption, most ideas languish. They never move beyond the Door to Engagement, which is why eight of ten new ideas, and nine of ten entrepreneurial ventures, struggle for significance.

I've been repeatedly exposed to the Segway since its release in 2001. The company's headquarters was in the building next to mine, until earlier this year when Segway, Inc. was sold to a U.K. company—yet my Door to Interest has remained closed to the idea. Channeling Homer Simpson: I understand the Segway. I just don't care.

The same is true of most struggling marketplace ideas—most restaurants, retail outlets, professional service firms, technology offerings, most everything. People understand, they just don't care—or they don't care enough.

THE LOCK

Here's the perceptual Lock: People like the myth of media exposure and persuasion. Whether or not you're aware of it, you probably do too.

It's pleasing and popular to imagine that you can create something and then message your way to success. Simply craft and deliver the right communication to the right audience—get them to understand—and eventually they *will* care, and your marketplace vision will become an everyday reality. It's an illusion.

It's undoubtedly true that short-term interest is peaked by novelty, media events, and gossip. After all, we like to pay attention to what others are paying attention to. But most short-term interest is driven by curiosity, not caring. It's like rubber-necking on the highway: Our minds don't *feel* that a discarded box or broken down car is worth pursuing. Rather, we feel compelled to take a look to see whether or not it is worth pursuing. And in most cases, it's not.

Take one of the most popular programs on television, *American Idol*. If it was a fact that awareness leads to interest and interest creates desire, *Idol*'s crowd-selected finalists would be swimming in platinum records (or at least gold).

Tens of millions of Americans tune in to watch *Idol* each week, and the program is broadcast to over 100 nations outside of the United States. *Idol*'s massive and targeted exposure to music lovers should fuel enormous desire and subsequent sales of the finalists' ideas, their music.

Unfortunately, it doesn't work that way. Just ask Taylor Hicks, Ruben Studdard, and Bo Bice.

Certainly the free entertainment idea called *American Idol* stimulates considerable desire and sales for *American Idol* (the show receives $16 million for each on air hour from attention-seeking ideas). But what about the companies that purchase *Idol*'s high-priced exposure in hopes it will create interest and stimulate desire for *their* ideas?

Ford Motor Co. has spent hundreds of millions of dollars sponsoring *Idol* over the years. Has that helped the company grow profitably during the new millennium? Where else could they have creatively invested those many millions to stimulate desire and open the Door to Interest to their quality vehicles? Where can you?

Like car brands, ideas are abundant today. And so is talent. What's in short supply is understanding. What wasn't understood by the aforementioned artists and the executives at Ford, and still isn't really understood by most, is that interest springs from desire, and not the other way around. Desire is the force behind every inquiry and every exchange.

Idol's third place finalist from Season 8, Milwaukee church music director Danny Gokey, was briefed on the power of desire courtesy of country music star Randy Travis. During his Hollywood work with *Idol,* Travis asked Gokey, "What about country; the fans would love and embrace you?"

Travis made meaning for Danny. He was telling Danny to tune *his* obsession to a specific *audience's* frequency, to *their* desires. He was hinting that Danny should embrace his passion, while keeping *those* people's desires deep in his heart.

Was Gokey enlightened? Time will tell. Are you enlightened? Have you figured out this marketplace brainteaser?

Consider Evian's roller-skating babies viral video, the most viewed online ad in history with over 100 million views. Despite its massive exposure, the video was *impotent* in its effect on sales of Evian's bottled water. People understood; they simply didn't care.

This confusion of behavioral cause and effect is the reason people continue to waste time and money on creative noise and navel gazing activities in the face of a rapidly changing and highly competitive environment.

It's why organizations place more and more emphasis and pressure on managing and measuring worn-out methods, instead of pursuing every opportunity and angle to be a bold and creative force in people's lives.

Great leaders, great entrepreneurs, and great marketers are not bamboozled by their brains. They're not misled by this myth—the self-involved, numbers obsessed, and persuasion-based view of the marketplace. They know that there's a more powerful, underlying reality behind unlocking the Door to Interest.

THE KEY

Here's the Key: Focus your attention and passion on your audience and their lives. Make every product, service, communication and interaction desirable ones . . . to them. Every single one.

Because the underlying reality of the marketplace is that it doesn't matter what people *think* about you or your idea. What matters is how your idea makes them *feel* about themselves, their private selves and public selves, their remembering selves, their experiencing selves, and their imagining selves.

Did your idea empower them? *Does* it make them feel smart? *Will* it connect them to others and help them be seen, heard, and appreciated?

Desire is an emotional thing. Desire is what makes the economy hum. Stop and look and you'll experience the vibrant and beautiful force of desire all around.

Neighbors mowing their lawns and washing their cars. Girls and boys putting on make-up and splashing on body fragrance. Children getting dressed for school. Fans on their way to a ballgame. Friends texting. Citizens voting. Entrepreneurs downloading software. Families heading to prayer service. Men and women browsing bookstore shelves, painting pictures, and tending gardens.

Desire is life. Life is desire. Lack of desire is clinically referred to as depression. Prolonged lack of desire by the masses is also called depression . . . by economists.

Desire is what gives us a sense of purpose and hope. Desire is what keeps us hungry, curious, and adventurous. You are currently experiencing desire, otherwise you wouldn't be reading this book.

Desire is also what fuels relationships. My desire for meaning and attention keeps me hopping on airplanes and hunting and pecking at the keyboard of my MacBook. I'm driven to help passionate people like you be the best they can be, for themselves and for others. Your desire for understanding and solutions, for control over your chaotic environment, drove you to choose this book.

Our desire for achievement and identity, our hunger to stand out and to make a difference, is what keeps us connected.

Demand is a Feeling

My university degree is in economics. Supply and demand.
Guns and butter. X/Y plots. The hard stuff. Thinking about it
now reminds me of something that George Bernard Shaw once
quipped, "If all the economists were laid end to end, they'd never
reach a conclusion."

I've reached a conclusion. My informed intuition, rich through
years of experience, confirms that demand is about the soft stuff.
It's not the curve on a graph. It's the feeling in someone's gut. It's
not a trend. It's a hunger.

We are *feeling*, then *thinking* people. Hearts, then minds. We
desire, all the time, and reason is simply a tool to help us advance
those desires. And so are you and your idea. Because it doesn't
work like this:

Westin Hotels. Who are we? What is our brand? *It's about us.*
What is our promise, personality, and positioning? *Us. Us.* What
do we want to say? How should we say it? *Us. Us. Us.* If only we
can discover our essence. If only we can get the message right
and get it across to everyone. *Us. Us. Us. Us.* Insight! New tagline!

It works like this:

I wonder who they are. *It's about them.* I wonder what they're
doing. *Them. Them.* I wonder how they're feeling. *Them. Them.
Them.* I wonder how we can make life better for them and make
them feel better about themselves. *Them. Them. Them. Them.*
Insight! The Heavenly Bed!

You don't find yourself; you create yourself through applied
energy and creativity. The Door to Interest is opened by con-

necting your idea to your audience's passions and hungers in a unique and attractive way, a way that fuels their desires and evokes a positive connection.

Desire is what animates the marketplace. Desire for control. Desire for attention. Desire for validation. Desire for contribution. Desire for excitement. Desire for status. Desire for belonging. Desire for a good night's sleep.

Desire is the stimulant. Desire is the Key that unlocks the Door to Interest.

Desire is the Ball

Don't take your eyes off of it. To unlock this Door, you must endlessly sense your audience's hopes, fears, and dreams and feed their emotional hungers. Become intimate with their lives. Develop a deep understanding of their circumstances. Fine-tune your empathy to their frequency. Walk in their shoes. Feel as if you live in their skin.

If you have questions or are feeling confused, get out of your office. Leave your store. Step away from the factory. Turn off your computer. Power off your smart phone, and saturate yourself and your idea into their daily grind. Find your audience's feelings deep inside yourself. Surround yourself with their sensibilities and expectations.

Then use your intuition, along with information and trusted guidance, and paint a unique and inspiring picture of the future. Make meaning, like Randy Travis did with Danny Gokey, and then bring that picture to life through your wild-eyed imagination and dogged persistence.

Serve

The first person served by service is the server. So serve them with all your heart. Your passion for them will lift you and sustain you. It will move you forward. It will embolden you. It will push you past doubt and resistance to breakthroughs. And it will keep the destructive and life-draining forces of arrogance and vanity at bay.

Success will inevitably turn to criticism. So if you value success, you must value criticism. I say, ignore both.

Every day is a day of opportunity to look beyond your to-do lists, spreadsheets and reports, and brighten the lives of those who need you. Commit yourself to uplifting and delighting others. Give them what they desire before they even know they want it. If you're not fanning the flames of desire each and every day, you are not doing your job.

Feed Their Hungers

Pretend the marketplace is a dark and confusing forest and your audience is bewildered and starving. Bewildered by the amount of choice and conflicting information, and hungry for attention and connection. Hungry for identity. Hungry for direction and meaning. How will you choose to lead them to your idea, the idea best designed to feed their hungers?

Will you spend your time and money handing out maps and stapling signs to trees? Or will you create a trail of increasingly larger breadcrumbs of value; ones that feed your audience's hungers and weave their way painlessly to a relationship with you?

Unlocking this Door isn't about manufacturing desires. It's about finding and feeding the ones screaming for sustenance. They're everywhere. They always have been, and they always will be.

In the 1960s, Volkswagen unlocked the Door to Interest of the younger generation by feeding their latent desire for frugality in car ownership, and by tapping into their need to display their rejection of the excesses of the older generation. The value of VW's 1960s idea (the Beetle) was inherent in the product's design—it was inexpensive to buy, run, and maintain—and it was famously brought to life with its clear and compelling advertising campaign.

Fast forward to the new millennium and Volkswagen's "Safe happens" campaign for its safe car idea—the Jetta. Again, VW brought the idea to life in an emotional and dramatic way. The shocking, car-crash ads were brilliantly executed—they were unexpected, communicated in an expressive manner, and were highly evocative of the value of the idea.

But, who valued the idea? Car safety wasn't in the hearts, or minds, of young car owners. It wasn't an itch that needed to be scratched, or a hunger for novelty or identity that longed to be satisfied. People's feelings are what point them in the direction of their desires. "Safe happens" was a manufactured direction. It was VW pointing—vivid in its depiction, yet sterile in its appeal.

By contrast, Apple's "I'm a Mac. I'm a PC." ads feed customers' hunger for identity. Pandora satisfies listeners' desire for novelty and self-expression.

Walmart connects with shopper's yearning to save time and money and, thus, feel smart. Target connects with those same shopper desires, yet weaves aesthetics into its idea reinforcing its audience's concept of self.

Amazon.com nourishes the need for knowledge and connection by enticing its audience to write reviews and rate Amazon offerings. Facebook, LinkedIn, and Twitter fuel the fascination with novelty and status, and feed the craving for attention and belonging.

Hyundai's extended warranties and assurance programs satisfy the longing for a sense of security and control. Tom's Shoes and Toyota's Prius feed the need for meaning and identity.

THE DESIGN

The Design of the Key to the Door to Interest is obvious yet hidden, since, as Goethe made clear, "The hardest thing to see is what is in front of your eyes."

Here's the Design: First, make everything that you say and do valuable to your audience. The great management philosopher Peter Drucker was *almost* right when he wrote, "What the business thinks it produces is not of first importance. What the consumer thinks he is buying, what he considers 'value' is decisive." It's what the consumer *feels* he is getting in exchange for his time, attention, and money that is decisive today.

Value is determined using an internal *feelings* calculator, with simple functions like add and subtract, right and wrong, and more complex ones like weighing the outcome of one's decision on future achievement, affiliation, and contribution.

Next, make sure that your idea is reflective of *their* idea, their idea of their past, present, and future selves. Make sure that your audience can clearly and proudly see themselves, their unique circumstances and ideal image, in everything that you say and in everything that you do.

Finally, focus on behavior. Desire springs more powerfully from our experiences than it does from our imaginations, especially our experiences with others. As the psychotherapist Milton Erickson made clear, "Change will lead to insight far more often than insight will lead to change." And change is the name of the game.

VALUABLE

Value is a complex and puzzling notion. Economists can't agree on a definition because it's not an objective concept. Value is multifaceted. Value is highly contextual. Value is subjective. Value is about desire. Value is delivered and imagined contentment, happiness, and self-worth. Value is an emotional thing. And whoever develops and delivers the best evolving composite of value, for their particular audience, wins.

Michael Porter, a leading authority on strategy and the competitiveness of nations wrote, "Strategy is about being different. It means deliberatively choosing a different set of activities to deliver a unique mix of value. Otherwise, a strategy is nothing more than a marketing slogan . . ."

Unlocking the Door to Interest is about your unique ability to imagine, create, and deliver a compelling and evolving bundle of value for your audience. It's holding a heap of potential and ideas in one hand and a wide range of "what would make people happy" in the other hand, and sorting and matching them to create surprising new combinations.

Value is Beyond Better

This isn't about being better. Better is something that can be rationally teased apart and quickly duplicated. This is about being different and unreasonable in ways, large and small, ways that assert integrity of purpose and add value to the lives of your audience. It's about being the best *for* them.

The iPhone is the best phone *for* Apple's audience, and it comes with a premium-price. The Flip video camera is the best *budget* device *for* theirs. Both are the best.

Being the best *for* is the only marketplace today that's not crowded. That's because the best widen the gap by doing more and more of what their audience desires and less and less of everything else. And that makes them stand out. It makes them irreplaceable.

Forget About the Other Guy

Value isn't about how to cleverly structure your business to beat the other guy. The competitive paradigm in business is another pervasive and misguided myth. It fosters imitation.

The word "competition" is from the Latin *competere*, meaning "seeking or striving together." The competitive paradigm forces you to compare yourself to, and align your thinking with, others. Others like you.

While Blockbuster Video was busy competing, being better *than* others like them, Netflix was busy being different in ways that were better *for* their customers.

Value is how you break away from others and stand out. It's about how you *irrationally* pour your heart, sweat and future into your idea and into the lives—and hands—of your audience.

Value isn't about one thing. So stop searching for that one thing. Value is a bundle of things, distinctive things that only you and the people you associate with can pull off. It's not about doing it once. It's about insatiable curiosity and passion, and being different over and over again for their benefit.

Unlocking this Door is about awareness, *your* awareness. Awareness that price matters because it makes us feel smart and feeds our identity hunger. Awareness that reputation and reliability matter because they make us feel secure. Awareness that design matters because it reflects our concept of self, to ourselves and to others.

It's also the awareness that selection matters, because the right amount of choice makes us feel in control. Empathy matters because it feeds our hunger for attention and recognition. Popularity matters because witnessing others using, wearing, and talking about an idea feeds our need to fit in and our desire to be right. And surprise matters because it engages us and lights up our novelty circuits.

In the past, "consumers" weren't really that interested in being surprised. They simply wanted quality, consistency, and reliability. Holiday Inn's slogan in the mid-70s was, "The Best Surprise Is No Surprise."

The quality bar has been raised and so have our expectations. Today, surprise matters . . . a lot.

Value is Subjective and Emotional

We're not rational creatures. We don't optimize our choices to survive in the most cost-effective and efficient manner possible. We buy to blossom. We select to show that we belong. We purchase to get a sense of control and meaning. We choose to avoid looking bad, as well as to draw attention. We decide in order to feel good.

Conventional wisdom, the notion of human beings as rational actors who are trying to optimize their marketplace decisions, drives people and organizations to dispassionately deconstruct and compare their objective idea to their competitors' ideas. Executives sit in endless meetings logically plotting their features, benefits, pricing, and positioning on 2 x 2 matrices.

But value isn't dispassionate. Value is an enthusiastic and creative exchange between people. Value isn't something you bring to life on your own. It's not inert matter that you can extract from the marketplace, like drilling for oil. Value is co-created. It's released through a mutually beneficial and stimulating relationship.

Kill the matrix. Kill complicated, time-consuming, and costly processes and engage people in possibility. Organize simple, powerful creative undertakings that produce a constant stream of ideas and meaningful activities. As Herb Kelleher, founder and former chairman and CEO of Southwest Airlines once remarked, "We have a strategic plan, it's called doing things."

In a world where everyone is busy trying to persuade us that their idea is the best idea—the best "value proposition" and the best "return on our investment"—it's the ones who drop breadcrumbs—the ones who "do things" to relentlessly feed our hungers and deliver unique and compelling value—who stand out. Today, creative execution *is* the strategy.

Great success is the product of a great passion, a passion for sweating the small stuff and adding value to every product, every service, and every interaction. Value delivered—value that causes people to become interested in an idea and feel proud about their decisions—is the meaning and purpose of any successful idea. Which begs a question: why are you doing what you do? Why are you doing "it?" Why do you create content? Why do you go to meetings? Why do you mail invoices? Why do you answer the phone?

If your answer is something other than, "I do it to add value, excitement and happiness to people's lives," then you're confused, at best.

Value is not some high-minded concept written up, printed, bound between covers, and placed on a shelf. Value is an attitude. Value is a vision brought to life by creative and caring human beings.

Value is about big acts of daring, and small acts of appreciation. Value is an elegant web application that's simple to understand and a pleasure to use. It's a beautifully designed envelope or invoice.

Value is a program that allows customers to opt-in to receive a text alert hours before your prices are scheduled to go up. It's a tweet that informs people that fresh, warm bread is exiting the ovens of their local bakery.

Value is also smart sourcing that brings new and affordable ideas to more people. It's inspired training and development that lights a fire in people and radiates that passion throughout the organization. Value is an enlightened hiring process that connects people to meaningful work that turns them on and, in turn, turns on others.

Value is a sparkling clean restroom. It's the points and "badges" awarded by online games. Value is rapid checkout and a cool shopping bag. It's a kind and caring agent who helps reroute a cancelled flight.

Valuable products and services are simply the table stakes today. Compelling value goes beyond the ante and asks, Is our email valuable? Is our logo? Our delivery truck? Is our brochure valuable? What about our web presence? Does our payment policy provide value? Our advertisements? Our packaging? Our signage? What about our sales presentation? Our dealer network? The tone of our voice? The smell of our lobby? The fire in our eyes? It then asks: Are they reflective?

REFLECTIVE

During the 80s, the great state of Texas was *litter*ally a mess. The state-maintained roads were strewn with trash, tossed predominately by eighteen-to-thirty-four-year-old males driving pickup trucks. Surprisingly, that willful cultural reality changed rapidly and dramatically with the genesis of a Texas Department of Transportation idea, an idea whose vital element epitomizes the next piece of this Design.

"Don't Mess With Texas," the longest-running and most successful antilitter campaign in history, was brilliantly conceived and brought to life by Austin-based advertising agency GSD&M. The agency smartly kicked-off the campaign by teasing their obstinate, litterbug audience in December of 1985, when bumper stickers with the words *Don't Mess With Texas* along side a small red, white, and blue Texas flag began surreptitiously appearing on pickup trucks. The heart of the idea was dramatically revealed soon after during the Cotton Bowl on New Year's Day, with a TV spot featuring legendary guitarist and Texas native son, Stevie Ray Vaughan.

The ad showed Vaughan, wearing his signature black gaucho hat and sitting on a stool on an empty stage in front of a huge Texas flag, slowly picking a moving rendition of the "The Eyes of Texas" on his Fender Strat. *"The eyes of Texas are upon you, All the live long day."* At the end of the song, the Texas blues virtuoso looked up and drawled, "Don't mess with Texas."

That one line, and the identity hunger it fed and desire it now evokes, has since been brought to life by Texas musicians, athletes, and celebrities including Lance Armstrong, Willie Nelson, George Foreman, and Leann Rimes. It appears almost everywhere in Texas—on t-shirts, coffee mugs, litterbags and bumper stickers —and University of Texas students even shout it loudly and proudly at sporting events. Why? What allowed this particular public awareness campaign to open a Door that others have found stubbornly locked? It was brilliantly reflective.

"Don't Mess With Texas" engaged its intended audience in an emotionally powerful, identity-focused and self-referential way by pitting proud Texans against them spineless litterers. The idea engaged people in a deep way by signaling further meaning. It fed Texan's identity hunger, allowing them to experience the emotional message in their mind's eye and make meaning for themselves.

People connect with what they internalize in their guts—what they desire and decide for themselves—not what they're told. Texans ability to visualize and internalize the community service plea in *their* terms is what opened their Door to Interest for the idea and motivated their behavior.

The British economist, John Kay wrote, "I am irresistible, I say, as I put on my designer fragrance. I am a merchant banker, I say, as I climb out of my BMW. I am a juvenile lout, I say, as I down a glass of extra strong lager. I am handsome, I say, as I don my Levi's jeans."

What do people internalize when they interact with you? What image does your idea help them conjure up about themselves?

Empathy not Persuasion

This isn't about persuasion, getting others to do what *you* want them to do. It's about demonstrated empathy. It's about molding your ideas to reflect *their* perceived interests and getting them to do what *they* want to do.

Did the antilitter campaign *persuade* Texans not to litter? No. The creative execution helped them reconstruct their reality and persuade themselves. Instead of announcing what the organization expected of them, it awakened Texan's own expectations.

Here's the bottom line: Your audience aches to believe that you "represent" them and that you're in it for, and with, them. Your ability to reach outside of yourself, and connect with them in a meaningful and reflective way, demonstrates this bond.

You're them. They're you. Connect your passion and purpose to their passion and purpose. Relate your unique view of the world and your place in it to their unique view of the world and their place in it. They long to see *themselves* and their unique needs in the reflection of your carefully polished idea. They crave your humble, yet confident and wide-eyed passion for the possible. They want you to display personality and to be vulnerable and human, like them. They want you to be a rebel with a cause.

What's more important to you? Selling yourself and your idea, so you can feed your hungers? Or bringing your idea to life in a way that feeds theirs?

Identity Thirst

Pepsi trails Coca-Cola in soft drink sales in just about every developed marketplace in the world, bar one. The one in which Pepsi artfully decided to feed its audience's profound thirst, while Coca-Cola stayed the course to feed their own.

In the 1970s, while Coca-Cola was busy connecting with Quebec's population through tried and true advertising featuring global icons like Michael Jackson, Pepsi changed course and started feeding Quebecers' nationalistic pride with commercials featuring local French-speaking celebrities, like Claude Meunier, a Quebec comedian.

In Pepsi's early slapstick commercials, Meunier's wacky characters —including a punchy hockey player—would spoof stereotypical Quebecers in their native dialects, highlighting their eccentricities, while enjoying a bottle of Pepsi. The ads creatively fed Quebecers' identity thirst and touched their hearts, and by association, fed their thirst for Pepsi.

Pepperidge Farm, a Campbell Soup Company brand, recently ran a smartly reflective print ad for its *Goldfish* crackers. The ad shows a large, smiling *Goldfish* cracker with its nose pressed gently against the nose of a much smaller, smiling *Goldfish* cracker. The headline reads: "We're bakers. But we're parents, too." In other, less expressive words, "We're like you. So we feel what you feel, and try to act as you would act."

Being reflective is not about creating spin. It's about spinning your focus, creativity and attention around to them. Thinking about your idea and bringing it to life in an honest, creative way, from *their* perspective. And it's not simply about modifying your verbal and visual communications. It's about the hardest thing in the world.

Einstein said, "The hardest thing in the world to understand is the income tax." But there's something much harder: To truly understand how another person is feeling, and to tune your passion, creativity, and activities to serve those feelings. It's making sure your idea is reflective of their desires. Your idea is reflective of their situations. Your idea is reflective of their hungers.

Reflective is a bank greeting each and every one of its customers by name. It's Pepsi changing its spelling to Pecsi in Argentina to accommodate the local idiom.

Reflective is the eco-nutrition label on Timberland's shoe packaging. It's the guttural roar of a Harley engine. It's the bud vase in a VW Beetle.

Reflective is Ben & Jerry's 2005 Earth Day protest against the opening of the Arctic National Wildlife Refuge to oil drilling by creating the largest ever Baked Alaska and placing all 1,140 pounds of it in front of the U.S. Capitol Building.

The more reflective—the more personal and meaningful—the less likely it will appeal to the masses and show up on your radar screen. And that's a good thing. Bill Cosby once said, "I don't know the key to success, but the key to failure is trying to please everybody." Being reflective is *ignoring* everybody and being one with your audience. It's about regarding them the way they regard themselves—as insiders, collaborators, and protagonists of the idea. It's feeding their spirit, giving them a sense of belonging and adding to their feeling of identity by being special and standing out.

Reflective helps people experience the most powerful feeling in the world, "It's not just me who feels this way. I am not alone."

BEHAVIORAL

The thought of eating cold, raw, dead fish used to disgust me. But now I eagerly head to a sushi bar at least once a month and gobble down morsels of hamachi, saba, sake, and kotate-gai. Being insatiably curious as to how people like me make decisions like that, I started thinking about precisely when and why I had altered my attitude of mind, and subsequently my life, in favor of the idea of cold, raw, dead fish. Had I seen an ad? Did I read an article or watch a cooking show? Did I bump into a Sashimi Facebook page or attend an event at Sashimi Stadium? Then I remembered: I hadn't altered my life by altering my attitude at all. What happened was precisely the opposite.

Around five years ago, after presenting to a group in Hawaii, I joined the host and participants for an early evening pupu party where ice cold beverages and a wonderful array of dishes were served: local favorites like guacamole and papaya-mango salsa, ahi seaweed salad with cucumber namasu, seared shrimp on a stick with hot wasabi cocktail sauce, and pineapple ice cream in chocolate cups.

There was also a chilled seafood bar and a passionate and skilled sushi chef. And it was during this alteration of my life that I experienced the clean flavors and beautiful presentations of Japanese sashimi, which forever changed my attitude . . . and my behavior.

Changes in Attitudes

People's attitudes about an idea are changed in two primary ways: through their active participation (behavior-induced) and through persuasion, where you use semantic and symbolic means to convince them to change.

Persuasion was a perfectly fine marketplace approach when people were predisposed to believe various claims, both overt and subtle ones, and when commercial messages were welcomed and consciously assimilated. But not so much today. The marketplace has changed.

Thirty years ago, the average American was targeted by around 500 daily commercial messages. Today that number is closer to 5,000. And people have changed with this changing marketplace reality; they're digitally empowered, much more marketing-savvy (and weary), and extremely distrustful.

That's why people increasingly employ message-blocking technologies and use Google as a message validation machine: "I wonder what others think of this idea?" "What have the outcomes been for people like me?" "What other alternatives are available." And so on.

But there is something they trust even more than Google. Something in which their confidence has never waned, especially when faced with an overwhelming amount of choice and information.

From Seven Cows to Number Three

In the early 1980s, Gary Hirshberg and Samuel Kaymen were churning out organic yogurt at their failing New Hampshire farm. As an upstart idea losing tons of money, it was critical for Stonyfield Farm to quickly make people aware of, and change their attitude toward, its organic products and values-based organization.

Even though people were still predisposed to messaging and persuasive appeals, the tiny company was forced, by limited resources, to focus on a more uncommon approach. They went to where people who shared and hungered for Stonyfield's values congregated, like Earth Day events and environmental rallies, and handed out cups of yogurt.

Luckily for them, that behavioral approach was all they could afford at the time. It helped break down the Door to Interest and Stonyfield has since grown in size, reputation, and credibility to become the number three yogurt brand in America.

As Hirshberg explained in a 2002 interview with *Reveries Magazine,* "People came away knowing not only that this was great yogurt, but also that Stonyfield is a company that truly cares."

Great organic yogurt (valuable), a company that truly cares about what its audience cares about *and* demonstrates it (reflective), and a cup and spoon placed directly into their hungry hands (behavioral).

Stonyfields' audience came to know, understand, and become interested—just as I came to know the wonderful experience of eating cold, raw, dead fish—through their personal experiences with the passionate people and exceptional products behind the idea. They came to know it from that one unbiased source that they know they can always rely upon: themselves.

It's much easier to make decisions based upon what influences you—reports, layouts, copy, media measurement, creative execution, etc.—but you must push to bring your idea to life in a way that looks and feels good to *them.* And in an age of hype, spin, and desperation, what looks good to people is increasingly a personally relevant experience that they can wrap their minds and hearts around.

As the philosopher and communication theorist Marshall McLuhan argued, it's "experience rather than understanding that influences our behavior."

Create an experience that reveals the vision and intention behind your idea. An experience that conveys look, feel, and, especially, meaning in a no spin, passionate way. An experience that allows people to alter their own attitudes of mind, without a hint of external persuasion. An experience that creates a motivation to act.

Behavioral is an engaging and meaningful conversation; one devoid of manipulation and overflowing with caring and concern. It's a trusted social platform where your audience can create, share, provide a helping hand and feed each others hungers.

Behavioral is also a complimentary chapter of a new book or a free song download from a new album. It's a loyalty card that feeds a powerful hunger with each use.

Behavioral is free and engaging content that brings people to your next meeting or to your website. It's an educational offering that draws your audience to your store or restaurant to try out your idea.

Context and Connection

If you want your idea to connect with people, you must weave it into their circumstances and situations in a finely-tuned way, in a way that makes sense and has meaning.

The interaction must be both relevant to your idea and desirable to them—in the moment they experience it; whether it is a piece of communication, a sample, or interaction with a human being.

Behavioral done right is Gillette giving samples of its disposable *Brush-Ups* teeth cleaners to airlines passengers soon after their in-flight meals. It's Canon inviting people to upload a photo to their website to try out a Canon printer. Canon then mails an actual print of the photo from the selected printer the very next day. It's Zappos letting people try on mail order shoes and then return them free of charge.

Behavioral is Starbucks *MyStarbucksIdea,* a website where people can submit and prioritize ideas for improving the Starbucks experience. It's Dunkin' Donuts' *Create Dunkin's Next Donut* contest.

When we're involved with something, we care. Behavioral is about inclusion and interaction; getting people to do things associated with your idea for *their* benefit. It allows them to feel connected to the idea. It causes them to internalize who they are and why they're doing what they do.

Behavioral opens the Door to Interest through *self*-influence.

DOOR TWO SUMMARY

The Door to Interest is the most perplexing of the three. Why? Because we can't see it. We've been conditioned to believe that our work is about transactions—making things, getting things done and making a buck (or two)—which acts as a kind of lens through which the entire world is perceived. Our eyes are unable to see our work in a larger, more empathic, and life-enhancing context. We simply don't believe that we're in the desire creation and fulfillment business. We haven't made the connection.

Open your eyes, and your heart, and make the connection. The winners in today's marketplace of ideas are those who focus on the feelings of others, those who feed the hungers of desire with unique interactions and experiences.

People want to enjoy the moment *and* see their future selves in a better place. If your idea is reflective and uniquely feeds their hungers, people will become interested and compelled to act.

Assuming they believe.

QUESTIONS TO ASK YOURSELF ABOUT
THE DOOR TO INTEREST

Are we deeply in touch with our audience's feelings and desires?

What audience hungers are we feeding? Are they their prevailing hungers? How do we know?

Are all of our activities valuable, in their eyes? If not, what can we do to make them valuable?

Are we stimulating desire in everything that we say and do? Or are we simply being helpful and nice?

Does our audience love our distinctive way of being? Can they see themselves and their unique desires and sensibilities reflected in our idea?

Are we still trying to persuade, or are we enticing our audience with creative and valuable experiences? Do the experiences reveal the vision, intention, and passion behind our idea?

On to the final Door.

DOOR THREE
Belief

We are all captives of the picture in our head—our belief that
the world we have experienced is the world that really exists.
—Walter Lippmann

It's extremely difficult to imagine the pictures in other people's
heads. As a consequence we become captives of our own beliefs
and allow our perceptions to influence our feelings and decisions
concerning others. Heaven knows I've banged my head in frustration on many locked Doors over the years—confident in my
point of view and approach, while blind to the inner world of
my audience.

Sometimes I wish I could go back and have a "do-over." Who
doesn't? But you can never go back. And some lessons simply
can't be taught. They have to be lived to be understood.

I lived one particular lesson that taught me more about unlocking
the Door to Belief than all the sage lessons found in books
and didactic talks ever could. It was a painful, yet enlightening
schooling.

I was working as CEO of a medical technology start-up and
presenting to the clinical staff of one of the most prestigious
teaching hospitals in the world. The meeting was arranged by our

distributor who had one of their sales people secure the meeting room, reproduce documents, set up the overhead projector, and order in lunch. At precisely noon, about a dozen physicians dressed in scrubs and with stethoscopes dangling from their necks, scampered into the room, plopped down at the conference room table and tore into their sandwiches.

After brief introductions, and while watching people chew, I launched into, what I believed to be, an engaging and informative demonstration of our idea for improving the lives of their patients. Sensing that my audience was anxious to get back to their work, I quickly segued into a detailed account of our FDA safety and effectiveness clearance, and summarized the results of our clinical trials. I was on fire! I didn't miss a beat (at least according to the song in *my* head).

As I closed my talk and proudly gathered up my notes and transparencies, someone at the far end of the conference room table called out my name.

"Mr. Asacker?"

I suddenly felt as if I had been transported back through time to the sixth grade. I glanced up and into the skeptical eyes of arguably the most deeply respected researcher in the field—the one individual who could single-handedly make or break our idea.

"Yes, Doctor," I replied, meekly. He then asked me a painfully rhetorical question.

"Are you the CEO of the company that developed this device?"

It was "rhetorical," because he knew darn well I was the CEO.

It was typed boldly at the top of everyone's agenda. "Painful" is what happened after I answered, "Yes, I am."

"And," he prodded. "You came to *our* teaching institution with such *shoddy* clinical data?"

I glanced from side to side into skeptical, staring eyes. My mind raced to create meaning and develop an appropriate response. I felt the blood drain from my face.

I knew there was nothing wrong with the data. We had spent months and a lot of investor money making sure the study was conducted at a reputable teaching hospital and with no outside influence. It was bulletproof. What could he be talking about?

Then it hit me! Our company had studied the *minimum* number of patients required for FDA clearance. As a cash strapped start-up, it was all we could afford (and just barely, at that). But, being a leader at one of the foremost institutions in the world, my protagonist, the good doctor, was used to *over-the-top* clinical presentations—thousands of patients studied and millions of dollars invested. In fact, large medical manufacturers used the sheer size of their studies—which were not necessarily more truthful, but were more reflective of their elite audiences—as barriers to entry for smaller firms like ours. They still do.

I was mentally backed into a corner. What was I supposed to do? Argue with his implied contention that more data was better data? Of course more data was better data. I was trapped. My heart began to race. My breathing became rapid. My awareness intensified. I began to see the world through a lens of fear. My very survival was on the line and I couldn't flee. So, I fought.

"Doctor," I uttered throatily, the words barely squeezing out of my larynx. "Do me a favor and turn to patient number seven." (The patient's names were removed from the studies to preserve confidentiality). As he flipped through the pages in his handout, everyone else in the room anxiously followed along in theirs.

"Do you see those squiggly lines?" I asked.

I was so upset that I smugly referred to critical physiological recordings as a child would—as "squiggly lines." He looked down at the data, then back up at me. I continued with my adrenaline-induced stream of consciousness.

"Those squiggly lines are Jim Olson. Jim lives in a little house in Maine. With a white picket fence. Two adorable little girls. And a wife who loves him. No one else could help Jim. Our product saved Jim's life."

I paused to catch my breath and then continued, pointing at him with a shaky finger and motioning to the other physicians around the table.

"And the minute numbers and squiggly lines mean more to you than people's lives, is the minute that you . . . and all of you doctors should get out of medicine." Yes, I really did say that.

I then stopped, picked up my documents, turned towards the door, and . . . my knees buckled. Sweat poured down my back. I fished the sales rep out from under a table where he had crawled to hide and walked out the door, wondering where I'd be working the following week.

Here's the peculiar after-effect of my apparent setback: That physician—who expressly and publically refused to be involved with medical companies, viewing it as a conflict of interest —agreed to sit on my company's medical board of advisors.

In addition, that story spread through our industry like wildfire. Whenever I'd walk into a hospital, the staff would ask, with Cheshire cat smiles, if I was the guy who told the doctors that if they didn't care about patients' lives, they should get out of medicine. I felt like a rock star.

In retrospect, I fully understand how my behavior brought about the desired effect—how it bulldozed down the Door to Belief. But at the time, I had absolutely no idea what I was doing or what was happening. My approach was haphazard and misguided. I was very lucky.

THE LOCK

Here is the Lock: You don't understand what's happening in the minds of your audience, either. You assume, like I did, that they believe in you and your idea. They don't. You are also under the impression that unlocking the Door to Belief is an analytical undertaking. It's about cleverly stating the facts and making well-reasoned arguments with adequate evidence. It's not.

After one of my recent speeches, an attendee approached me and made an important and significant distinction about marketplace ideas, "Unless it can make a difference in my life," he said. "It's a waste of my time." When people become overwhelmed with life, like they are today, they tune out everything that appears superfluous. They focus only on those ideas that they *feel* will help them with *their* work and *their* lives.

That same distinction applies to the Door to Belief. Unlocking it goes well beyond getting people to believe that you are who you say you are, and that your idea works the way you say it does. It goes deep, into the essence of your idea.

Be aware of this reality: People do *not* believe you. What they believe is what they tell themselves about your idea from the signals they receive. And ultimately, they choose their beliefs by what *difference* the idea will make in their lives.

Realize this as well: The day your idea stops being purposeful and meaningful, or ceases to have people's best interests at heart, is the day they'll replace it with something else.

THE KEY

Here's the Key: Be real. When I finally composed myself and deconstructed my edifying hospital experience, I realized that my *scripted* presentation was the furthest thing from real; it was logical and lifeless. I approached it the same way I handled our FDA submission: I rationally designed it to *convince* the decision makers to believe in my idea by *comparing* it to the others they were familiar with. Instead of being a rebel with a cause, I was a suit with an agenda. Instead of being passionate and real, I was cool and reasonable.

My presentation should have been a statement about what I believed in and what life should be about, for them and their community. I should have been focused on *their* desire for meaningful *change*—a change in their lives, as well as in the lives of their patients. I should have fed their hungers. I should have inspired them to *care*.

Luckily, something inside me snapped and the "real me" finally showed up. But I would never recommend that impulsive, very risky and taxing approach. Instead, take a page out of the book of the passionate James Trevor Oliver.

Reality Hunger

Jamie Oliver, chef, author, and restaurateur, is transforming the way we feed ourselves and our children. He's doing it by combining his love of food and cooking with a warm, entertaining, and candid approach to his work, and by using substance and theatre to bring his idea to life. Jamie is changing the way we eat by being real.

I first became aware of Jamie from his appearance at a TED Conference (Technology, Education, Design). Here's how he described his idea during his acceptance speech for the $100,000 TED Prize in early 2010:

"My wish is for everyone to help create a strong, sustainable movement to educate every child about food; inspire families to cook again; and empower people everywhere to fight obesity."

Jamie's cause is certainly a noble and worthy one. But there are many who are dedicated and driven by that same idea. What makes Jamie's vision so inspiring? What has allowed a 34-year-old Briton to capture and maintain the imagination and interest of millions? Jamie Oliver—his unique character and how he brings his idea to life in an engaging, interesting, *and* believable way. And there's no better example of precisely how he's gone about it, than that inspiring TED award speech in Long Beach, California.

The youthful, London-born chef stepped onto the stage and began his presentation by connecting to the reality of the moment with an expressive, specific, and contextually relevant statement:

"Sadly, in the next 18 minutes when I do our chat, four Americans that are alive will be dead from the food that they eat."

Then, after briefly introducing himself, Jamie candidly and humbly explained that he had been working tirelessly over the past seven years to save lives, but in his own way.

"I'm not a doctor. I'm a chef. I don't have expensive equipment, or medicine. I use information . . . education. I profoundly believe that the power of food has a primal place in our homes . . . that binds us to the best bits of life."

He went on to engage his audience and bring his idea to life with broad, emotional questions, as well as singling out individuals to make his idea more vivid and real. He displayed grim statistical data about our diet-related disease state and its consequences, while injecting bits of compassionate humor that kept his audience happy and hopeful, feeling confident and in control.

And he told stories—emotionally powerful stories about real people, and their very real and heartbreaking challenges.

Here's how Jamie introduced stories from his journey to Huntington, West Virginia—considered to be the unhealthiest and most obese city in America; an experience that was captured on film and went on to become the hit, prime-time television show, *Jamie Oliver's Food Revolution.*

"I want to introduce you to some of the people that *I* care about; your public . . . your children."

Jamie continued his passionate rant with heartrending photographs, enlightening video clips, and vivid, meaningful stories. He even brought one story to life by pouring a wheelbarrow full of sugar cubes onto the stage.

Jamie understands the power of theatre and of humanizing his idea. He also understands that belief isn't about transferring knowledge. Belief is about bringing an idea to life in a real and meaningful way and inspiring people to care. Because when people *don't* care, when they're not emotionally invested, they get analytical and start *comparing* ideas. And comparing often leads to a non-decision, or a decision based primarily on cost.

This explains why one of the West Virginia schools Jamie was trying to help was ambivalent about his recommendations. The staff continued to *rationally* compare processed chicken nuggets to fresh chicken for their students' meals, ultimately choosing to continue with the slightly less expensive and less healthy nuggets. They simply didn't care. Not enough, anyway. Sure, they understood Jamie's argument. But they didn't believe enough in the difference it would make in their lives and in their children's lives. In their minds, and hearts, the products were "comparable," which made it a relatively trouble-free "features and pricing" decision.

Don't allow yourself to be comparable. Don't be "like" others. Knowledge may inform, but it's feelings that motivate. Give your audience meaning and value that compels them *not* to compare. Compel them to believe—in your integrity of purpose, in your imaginative vision, and in your unique value and personality. And you do it . . . by being real.

Be the Proof

Jamie Oliver is living proof of his idea, an idea saturated with conviction and passion. He talks the talk *and* walks the walk. It's his behavior that builds belief. Are you committed to your idea? Do you behave in a passionate and congruent way? Are you living proof? Are your people? Do you stay true to your unique view of the world and your place in it?

How passionately do you believe in your idea? How far would you go to demonstrate your conviction, to prove your point? Would you gulp down a glass teeming with *Helicobacter pylori* bacteria?

In 1981, Australian researcher Barry Marshall believed so passionately in his and fellow researcher Robin Warren's radical idea that bacteria, not stress, caused stomach ulcers that he proved it to the disbelieving medical establishment by drinking a glass filled with hundreds of millions of *H. pylori* bacteria.

Using an endoscope, his research team monitored the progression, antibiotic treatment, and eventual cure of Marshall's severe gastritis, moving his revolutionary idea forward in the world of ulcers and gastrointestinal medicine. Years later their world-changing idea would become common knowledge. And as a tribute to their conviction and tenacity, both men were eventually awarded the Nobel Prize in medicine.

It's difficult *not* to believe someone who drinks a concoction overflowing with harmful microorganisms. Be difficult *not* to believe. I'm not asking you to risk your life (although that may be the cost of someone's unwavering commitment to an idea). I'm simply asking you to eat your own dog food. I'm asking you to love your idea. I'm asking you to be passionate about the integrity of your purpose. I'm asking you to refuse to compromise your beliefs.

Ask yourself, do all of our actions convey our passion and conviction to our idea? And if not, ask why not?

Belief is in the Details

Jerry Murrell is one of the founders of Five Guys Burgers & Fries, a 570-store fast food restaurant chain with annual sales approaching $500 million. In a 2010 interview with *Inc. Magazine*, Jerry expressed his conviction for his idea—specifically the value of Five Guys' food—by describing various decisions his company has made.

According to the article, unlike most fast-food restaurants that serve dehydrated frozen french fries, Five Guys uses fresh potatoes, which go through an elaborate soaking and pre-frying process. In addition, their potatoes are sourced from Idaho, aiming specifically for baking potatoes "grown north of the 42nd parallel," even though "it would be a lot easier and cheaper if we got a California or Florida potato."

One time, Jerry and his team were challenged with a choice, to care or compare. Five Guys' prices are based on margins, which means they raise or lower their prices based solely on their food costs. One year, hurricanes destroyed the tomato crops in Florida, which resulted in a large cost increase to Five Guys. To preserve their margins, a few of Five Guys' franchisees contacted corporate with a decision to stop offering tomatoes on their hamburgers. Jerry made a quick and *rational* executive recommendation: Use *one* slice of tomato instead of two.

Here's how Jerry described his sons'—the four other guys and owners—reaction to his proposal:

"My kids were furious: 'It should be two! Always!' They were right—it's too easy to start slipping down that slope. We stuck with two slices, and so did our franchisees."

Instead of deciding to compare, to rationalize, Jerry decided to care. And, as a result, so did the people around him. Being real is deciding to care. It's staying true to the heart and soul of your idea. Being real is being fanatical and consistent in every decision, public and private. Being real is taking pride in your idea and sweating the details.

Being real is also sweating the financial implications of those details, like a slice of tomato or, in the case of Pixar Animation Studios, the appearance of cartoon cheese.

In 2005, half way through the production of their animated film *Ratatouille*, the amazing storytellers at Pixar replaced director Jan Pinkava with Brad Bird. And even though they were on an extremely tight budget and behind schedule, Bird stopped production and spent millions of dollars and many months working to perfect . . . Are you ready for this? . . . the appearance of the cheese and the stance of Remy the rat. Months and millions on a cartoon rat and cartoon cheese! That's passion. That's caring. And that created one of Pixar's most acclaimed films to date.

Gloria Steinem wrote, "We can tell our values by looking at our checkbook stubs." Take a look at your checkbook stubs. Where do you invest? When do you take a stand? What matters most to you? What do you value?

THE DESIGN

Of all three Doors, the Design of the Key to this one has changed the most over the past fifty years. Today's skeptical and savvy consumers, inundated with new ideas shouting at them every day, have changed how they screen for relevance and credibility.

Not long ago, unlocking the Door to Belief was a pretty straight-forward undertaking. All an idea needed was looks, credentials, and proof points. Today, every idea looks good. Everyone has a fancy package and website. Everyone is an expert. Everyone has followers. Everyone has an elevator speech. Everyone has testi-monials. And, thanks to the Internet, everyone can tell a story to anyone else. So what's next?

Here's the Design: First, make sure your idea is vivid to your audience. The more direct, visual, and specific something is, the more believable. Bring your idea to life, in their mind's eye, in a visually powerful, clear and memorable way.

Next, work to make your idea tangible. Make its distinctive value visible in the real world. It's the theatre *and* substance of your idea that differentiates and makes it believable. Bring your idea to life through your bold and congruent actions.

Finally, make your idea social. Make it come alive and be seen and heard in the world of your audience. We are social creatures and are highly susceptible to the actions and behaviors of others. Our brains are wired for connection. So, give people something valuable that they can identify with and share with others.

Remember, belief is subjectively created from people's perception of your idea, its character, behavior and popularity. It's their experience that builds belief, not your intentions or promises.

The English playwright and Oscar winning screenwriter Robert Bolt wrote, "A belief is not merely an idea the mind possesses; it is an idea that possesses the mind."

VIVID

Were you one of the lucky ones to snag Apple's iPad when it was first released? Tom Dickson was and, in his fanatical pursuit of publicity, he rushed back to his office and videotaped himself smashing, folding, and destroying it.

Dickson is the founder of Blendtec, an industrial blender manufacturer in Orem, Utah. In a bold effort to bring his idea to life in a vivid way, Tom has been blending and pureeing tech gadgets and household objects such as golf balls, garden rakes and cell phones, and posting the videos on YouTube for all to see (and pass around).

His quirky theatrical series, *Will it Blend?*, has been viewed by tens of millions, won numerous marketing awards, and is trumpeted as an example of the power of social media for viral marketing.

Unlike the Evian roller-skating babies viral video, Dickson's *Will it Blend?* idea created belief—it got people to say, "Wow! Blendtec sure does make a powerful blender!"—and, as a result, helped the company increase sales more than tenfold in four years.

Dickson's *Will it Blend?* videos work as a kind of cognitive and emotional shorthand. They're essentially short stories—with a setting, a protagonist, conflict, and, eventually, a climax (usually dust and smoke)—that instantly transmit belief by allowing people to get caught up in the idea and make the meaning for themselves.

Belief is Emotional

Think back to your last encounter with a salesperson. What was it like? Can you recall a recent advertisement? Describe it. Or how about the last meeting you attended or email you read?

My guess is that they were pretty much fact-filled and uninspiring, which means that, by and large, they were ineffective at creating belief. No engagement, no visualization. No visualization, no personal, emotional impact. No emotional significance, no change in belief. Simple. We believe what we internalize, what we *feel* and decide for ourselves, not what we're told.

According to a recent study, a television drama may be more effective in getting young women to believe in and use birth control than a news-format program on the same issue. Why? Because the message was in a format that the women liked. They viewed the characters as friends, not authority figures. The message was subtle, not overt. They didn't feel they were being told how to behave. People are more deeply influenced by narrative laced with details and emotion, than by methodical lectures and mounds of data. Story is also an especially effective approach in today's multimedia world, where attention spans continue to shrink and information overload forces people to simplify.

Am I suggesting that you run out and buy a video camera? Yes, if you're ready to do the hard work of using it to make your idea interesting and truthful. What I am really asking you to do is to be lively and transparent, and give people the details they need to convince themselves. I'm asking you to be a bit more like Gary and Hugh.

Garyvee and Gaping Void

Gary Vaynerchuk, "@garyvee" on the social media platform Twitter, is the 31-year-old co-owner, with his Russian-immigrant parents, of a wine retail shop in Springfield, New Jersey. Hugh "Gaping Void" MacLeod is a 44-year-old, burnt out New York ad copywriter turned cartoonist and new media consultant, presently residing in Alpine, Texas.

Vaynerchuk's online wine tasting show, *Wine Library TV,* is viewed by hundreds of thousands and has been featured in *The Wall Street Journal, Time Magazine* and on *The Ellen Degeneres Show.* MacLeod's blog, *Gaping Void,* draws a million plus visitors each month, and is a must-read of the digerati and creative types of every ilk.

Both men brazenly come from a place of truth, and both have used vividness, along with a healthy dose of self-promotion and social networking savvy (to feed their audiences' hungers) to become microcelebrities.

Vaynerchuk brings his idea of the down-to-earth wine connoisseur to life through frequent video podcasts from a table in the corner of his cluttered office above the family wine store. His deep knowledge and spot-on nose combined with his hyperactive on-screen delivery and frequently outrageous metaphorical descriptions, demystifies the complex and makes his wine tasting reviews a valuable, vivid and believable experience for his audience.

MacLeod's idea of the rebellious creative comes to life through a constant stream of entertaining anecdotes and insightful thoughts on his blog, and through his recurrently cheeky (okay, profane) and very popular cartoons. Vaynerchuk uses video. MacLeod uses keyboard and pen. Both entrepreneurs creatively combine their passions and authentic voices in an entertaining and spirited way.

I've heard it said that the likelihood that you're right is not increased by the intensity of your conviction. True enough. But it sure does enhance belief.

Wine sales at Vaynerchuk's store have exploded since launching his vivid and engaging video blog. And MacLeod's cartoon business is booming. Both men have even leveraged their substantial, hard-earned audiences to land book deals with major publishing houses.

Vivid isn't about the tool. And it's not simply about creating content. It's about intensity of conviction, and bringing your idea to life in a human, imaginable, and memorable way. Vivid is about the truth. It's about your truth and it's about their truth.

Can You Handle the Truth?

Years ago I studied magic with one of the most knowledgeable and skillful practitioners in his field. The guy would spend hour upon hour perfecting the most novel illusions and esoteric sleights. In fact, he had become so expert at his art that he even fooled most professional magicians. He was, technically, the "best." And he remains a virtual unknown.

The "fact" was the quality of his magic was beyond compare, but the facts didn't matter much to his audience. What mattered to them was how they were feeling during his performance—their "truth." And their truth was that they were less interested in his technical skill and more interested in being entertained.

Most of us act like my magical friend. We push the facts—the features, attributes and quality of our idea, while ignoring the truth—the feelings of our audience. We focus on the rational and measurable, and disregard the emotional and ethereal. An idea is never more than a means to an end. And that end, that truth, is always a feeling. It's the feeling that draws people in. We want to get lost in your idea. We want to *feel* the importance and meaning of what you offer—for ourselves, in our guts. We don't want to be objectively convinced. We want to subjectively believe.

Being vivid is about tapping into that truth and exciting people's imaginations. It's also about feeding people's hungers to understand and to be right. It's about satisfying both their impulsive minds *and* their immersive ones.

Impulsive and Immersive

Think of your idea as a big jigsaw puzzle. Some people will build a meaningful and believable picture with only a few vivid pieces, like witty prose and an engaging video. Others will require many more pieces, both big and small, like detailed analyses and access to customer reviews. Your job is to make *all* of those pieces available to your audience.

Think about how *you* choose marketplace ideas. Do you research an idea before you make your final choice? How extensively? Do you desire social interaction with the people behind those ideas? How much? It depends, right? If the idea matters to you, you might read the label and check out a few online customer reviews. If it matters a lot, if the idea plays a significant role in some aspect of your life, you'll dig deep in pursuit of the inside story, comparative data and specialized knowledge. You may even spend time interacting with other like-minded people.

Sports nuts, computer geeks, dog lovers, wine aficionados, outdoor enthusiasts, bibliophiles, car buffs, foodies, and other category experts are highly discriminating and demand deep knowledge and immersive experiences. More casual or impulsive decision-makers simply want supporting evidence and, in fact, may become confused or frightened by too much choice and information. All play devil's advocate with themselves, looking for signals to help rationalize their feelings and make the "best" possible choice. So what should we do?

Simple. Give people the signals they seek. Appeal to their emotionally sensitive, impulsive minds by creating powerful visual stories and metaphorical associations. And satisfy their more literal, immersive minds by providing relevant details and connections to others like them.

But don't push your proof on people. It will work against you. Various studies have shown that the more information people are *given* about a subject, the less engaged they become. In addition, people tend to *harden* their beliefs when confronted with facts that challenge them. Instead, allow those who *want* more information to get it when, and how, they desire it. Make the information easy to find, easy to follow, and easy to swallow. Stimulate their imaginations, and then feed their hunger to understand and their desire to be right. Think through, and *feel*, each and every question someone may have about your idea and provide access to a direct, vivid and compelling answer. Because today, one unanswered question, one inconsistency, is enough to make people turn away.

Interesting and Truthful

The great playwright and film director David Mamet wrote, "It is the writer's job to make the play interesting. It is the actor's job to make the performance truthful."

Vivid is about being both writer and actor. It's about creating dramatic scenes that help people visualize and internalize your idea, *and* keeping them interested with meaningful and evolving details.

For an awe-inspiring example of how to bring an idea vividly to life, look no further than the National Football League; an idea that has surprisingly surpassed baseball as America's favorite pastime.

U.S. football is a raw, dirty, tedious block-and-tackle game. If you've never played, you probably can't appreciate the distinction between the game as it exists in reality and how it comes to life for the benefit of the television audience. Trust me when I tell you: TV football is nothing like the gridiron.

It's a testimony to the creativity of the NFL, and its understanding of vividness, that its idea bears little resemblance to my memory of playing the actual game. In a three-hour televised game, there are about 11 minutes of actual football. The rest is theatre, and layer upon layer of detail.

The NFL employs a vast array of cameras, a constant flow of information to the camera crew, quick cuts, reaction shots, dramatic storytelling, and play-by-play analysis at the molecular level. In essence, it has created an alternate reality.

And that's true of all great marketplace ideas. Vivid is about taking the common, the reality, and making it uncommon. It's about taking the simple facts and turning them into a compelling truth.

What allows professional athletes of all stripes to reap the marketplace rewards of millions of dollars? Someone else's unique ability to bring those games to life, in a vivid way for the benefit of the viewing audience.

Vivid is a "package" that makes you long for what's inside, with a "label" that answers your most gnawing question. It's a landing page with an engaging video of an idea in use, along with links to unedited customer reviews.

Vivid is the classic advertising headline penned by David Ogilvy in the late 50s: "At 60 miles an hour the loudest noise in this new Rolls-Royce comes from the electric clock."

It's the brush-bottomed, anthropomorphic bubbles that dramatize S.C. Johnson's *Scrubbing Bubbles* bathroom cleaner idea. It's those expressive and evocative iPod billboards with the silhouetted, dancing hipsters.

Vivid was Orson Welles' 1938 radio news broadcast adaptation of *The War of the Worlds,* which created widespread panic. It was JFK's 1961 "Man on the moon" speech, which ignited a dream.

Vivid *is* last year's Academy Award–winning film, *The Hurt Locker*, which unequivocally affected viewers' beliefs about war.

Vivid is writing that stirs the imagination. It's a friend's emotional story that draws you in. It's a diagram or chart that makes the essence of an idea crystal clear. It's an intense sensory experience that ignites a fire in your mind.

Vivid is a dream. Vivid is a force that moves and inspires. Vivid affects belief through perception. And perception is truth, but *only* in the absence of a meaningful, personal experience.

TANGIBLE

Aaron Levenstein wrote, "Statistics are like a bikini. What they reveal is suggestive, but what they conceal is vital." The same is true of marketplace ideas. Vividness reveals a suggestive idea. It draws people in with personality, drama, and a unique point of view. It opens doors. But it's the substance of the idea that keeps those doors open.

Window dressing can create engagement and interest, but people buy what's inside. They adopt and share ideas that are real; those that reveal their true selves through their fresh and relevant actions, and that treat their audience as partners in an exciting and evolving game of experience co-creation. Today, it's what you *do* that matters most.

Tangible actions make people realize that somebody cares about *their* experiences. Tangible expresses the point of your idea, your ethos and purpose. Tangible is your soul. And it's that authentic and dynamic spirit that truly motivates.

The Soul of the Idea

Starbucks was a soulful idea that came to life through a passion for premium-blend coffee *and* a carefully orchestrated atmosphere. But as it grew, the tangible attributes that brought Starbuck's idea fully to life—like the cool, comfy couches, the hand-pulled shots, the aroma of fresh ground coffee, and the doting baristas—were "streamlined" to support rapid growth.

And as the tangible attributes slowly melted away, so too did customers' belief in the Starbucks idea. As Starbuck's chairman and CEO Howard Shultz made very clear in an internal company memo in 2007, "Stores no longer have the soul of the past."

Tangible is about the soul of your idea. It's about making decisions and choosing behaviors that bring that soul to life in the hearts and minds of your people, and in the real world for the benefit of your audience. Tangible is about who you are *through* what you do, both small acts of caring and bold strokes of creation.

Mark Twain once pointed out, "Actions speak louder than words, but not nearly as often." Tangible is about speaking your beliefs *through* your inspired actions. There's an old Wall Street saying, "To know and not to do is not to know." It's also true that to *feel* and not to do is not to feel. To feel concern is to show concern. To feel connection is to create connection. To feel a clear sense of identity and purpose is to live and breathe a clear sense of identity and purpose.

Take Toyota. The soul of its idea—the tangible reliability and longevity of its vehicles—steadily opened the Door to Belief and helped the company grow into the world's biggest automaker. Belief in that idea suffered a recent setback due to record recalls and a publicity nightmare that culminated in Akio Toyoda, president of Toyota and grandson of the company's founder, testifying in front of the U.S. House Committee on Oversight and Reform.

During the proceedings Toyoda remarked, "My name is on every car." His statement was intended to convey belief, belief that, as a leader, nothing was more important to him than his customers. After all, a car idea is only as strong as its customers' feelings for the idea. Unfortunately, that simply wasn't the case.

In the past, Toyoda said, the company's priorities were safety and quality, and sales came last. But, he explained, as Toyota grew to become the world's biggest carmaker, "these priorities became confused, and we were not able to stop, think and make improvements as much as possible."

Sure they were. It was a choice. Like every organization, Toyota could have chosen to stop, think and make the right decisions. They chose not to. By confusing the essence of his business with the numbers that essence produced, by turning Toyota's obsession away from tangible quality and reliability to sales and profitability, Akio Toyoda may have unwittingly locked the Door to Belief that took his people four decades to crack open.

Akio Toyoda is not alone in this misguided business approach; this rigid, inside-out focus on the organization and its "numbers." We're witnessing many leaders losing their sense of empathy and becoming narcissistic; obsessed with their image as reflected by internal goals and measurements, popularity polls and opinions of experts and analysts.

I've said it before, and I'll say it again and again: Business is not about numbers. It's about culture and feelings. It's a way to help people; to fuel prosperity and well-being. Numbers simply tell you how well you're doing with those feelings with the tangible contribution you're making to people's lives.

Why did so many people buy Toyota vehicles (me included)? Because we believed. We believed that the people at Toyota were obsessed. We believed that they cared deeply about us and our cars. We believed that they were passionately committed to the truth and to the pursuit of perfection. And so, we felt cared for and safe. But then we found out that, indeed, they were obsessed. But, like so many businesses today, they just weren't obsessed with us.

Are you obsessed with your audience? Are you obsessed with your idea? Or are you obsessed with yourself, your problems, your messaging, and your numbers? What is the soul of your idea?

Integrity of Purpose Creates Belief

Like Starbucks and Toyota, Southwest Airlines has grown rapidly—from a regional upstart with three aircraft in 1971, to the largest and most profitable airline in the world. It's done it by being obsessed with the details, and with the tangible results those decisions deliver to customers.

In 2009, U.S. airlines earned close to $3 billion in baggage fees. While that very tangible industry pursuit was underway, Southwest Airlines' CEO, Gary Kelly, was drawing criticism from Wall Street analysts by staying true to the essence of the Southwest idea and continuing to allow customers to check bags for free. Southwest felt its customers' desires and *substantiated* those feelings through its actions. The result? Belief. According to Kelly, that tangible demonstration of the Southwest idea resulted in an additional $1 billion in annual market share and $11 million in earnings for the first quarter of 2010, one year after the airline lost $91 million.

Kelly's decision was a difficult one. Meaningful decisions always are, because the rational mind demands to know, "Will it pay off? When? Are you sure?"

A slice of tomato, the stance of a cartoon rat, "Bags Fly Free," all appear, at first glance, to be fairly insignificant decisions. In fact, they were defining choices that cost a great deal of time and money. More importantly, all required creativity and courage, an instinct to produce, and passion for the possible. And they all created the most important asset known—belief.

Belief is Created, Not Communicated

"If you want people to think you're funny, don't *tell* them you're funny. Tell them a joke."

You've heard it many times, but few practice it. Why not? Because joke *writing* requires creativity, time, and effort. It's not easy to create something original and compelling. And joke *telling* takes guts. Unfortunately, energy and creativity are what it takes to forge closer connections and separate your ideas from the scores of others in today's saturated marketplace.

Today's consumers are weary and wary of marketplace promises. They're hungry for reality. They're aching to believe in you and your idea and to experience the inspired creations of intelligent, playful, and caring human beings.

The days of buying attention and *communicating* belief are on life support. Today you *earn* belief through the tangible details of your offering and the inspired actions of your people.

Belief is created through caring. Nordstrom has become legendary for its tangible acts of compassion. It has been known to unquestioningly accept returns, pay customers' parking tickets, send tailors to customers' homes, and even lend cash to strapped customers. How have you demonstrated caring today?

Belief is created through attention to detail. As the story goes, Conrad Hilton, the founder of Hilton Hotels, was asked at a celebration of his life for the single, most important lesson he'd learned during his long and successful career. He replied, "Remember to tuck the shower curtain inside the bathtub." What small yet significant detail did you attend to today?

Belief is created through innovation. Walt Disney once said, "We keep moving forward, opening new doors, doing new things because we are curious, and curiosity keeps leading us down new paths." What new doors have you opened lately?

Your relationship with your audience is based on nothing more than belief. Their belief in your ability to continuously surprise them, feed their hungers and make them feel proud of their association with you and your passionate belief that you can.

Focus on your idea. Have an ambitious purpose and understand the tangible issues that will ultimately make the greatest difference to your people and to your audience. Then look at what you do, why you get out of bed in the morning, as an opportunity to stand out and rise above the growing sea of sameness by doing something distinctive, meaningful, and emotional.

Belief is emotional. Belief happens by speaking to people's feelings.

People's behavior is reinforced when you help them feel good about their, mostly, subconscious and habitual marketplace choices. Tangible actions create those feelings.

Tangible creates a *feeling* of neighborliness. It's a bank that's open when it's most convenient for *you*. It's an auto dealer's free pickup and delivery service when performing maintenance on your car.

Tangible creates a *feeling* of belonging. It's walking into a specialty foods store and getting the feeling that you've walked into someone's kitchen. It's a bartender remembering your name and favorite drink.

Tangible creates a *feeling* of being cared for. It's a cell phone provider calling to let you know that you're about to exceed your usage limit, and then providing extra minutes free of charge. It's a large, toll-free number and a "chat now" feature on every page of a company's website.

Tangible creates a *feeling* of liking. It's Geek Squad's funky attire and vehicles. It's a fast-food restaurant encouraging customers to play "Rock, Paper, Scissors" with the cashier to win a dollar off their purchase.

Tangible creates a *feeling* of appreciation. It's a confident and caring financial advisor calling during bad times and thanking you for your belief in her. It's a consultant passing on highly relevant connections and ideas to help save you time and money.

Tangible creates a *feeling* of warmth. It's Doubletree Hotels proffering a freshly baked chocolate chip cookie at check-in, regardless of the hour. It's Ben & Jerry's "Free Cone Day."

Tangible creates a *feeling* of being understood. It's finding the operating instructions to your new product on the company's website. It's a radio station cutting back on the number of ads and making the others more interesting and relevant.

Tangible *proves* who you are and what you believe. Tangible is U.S. Cellular's elimination of cell phone contracts for its loyal customers. It's the bags of potatoes stacked high in Five Guys' restaurants, and the extra helping of fries they *purposefully* add to each order. It's Sun Chips' biodegradable bag.

Tangible is an aspiring performer hopping up on stage and doing her unique and passionate thing over and over again, gratis. It's someone showing emotionally honest and open behavior, speaking the unspoken with candor and compassion.

Tangible is about being proud of your idea and demonstrating uniqueness through your actions. But tangible actions are not simply about your offering. They also communicate your philosophy, your unique view of the world. Tangible actions create belief in your idea *and* your ideals.

Tangible is Procter & Gamble sending thousands of bottles of Dawn to help animals affected by the oil spill in the Gulf of Mexico. It's Walmart's "Fighting Hunger Together" initiative, which provides $2 billion in cash, food, and logistical expertise to the nation's food banks over the next five years.

Tangible makes you think, "Wow! They *are* different." Tangible makes you believe. And so do the actions of others.

SOCIAL

Last fall my aunt traveled from her native Louisiana to visit my family. As we drove from the airport toward my home, her eyes became large as they devoured the brilliant golds and reds of a New England autumn. It was an unexpected and exciting experience for her.

Later that day, I decided to take a walk in the woods to find some vibrant, pristine leaves that she could press and take back home. I tossed on my barn coat, grabbed a paper sack, and headed down a well-worn path overflowing with recently fallen leaves. As I walked along, with my eyes fixated on the ground attentively searching for the perfect leaf, all I could see were decay and various shades of brown. I could not believe that in an area overflowing with foliage, I couldn't find one leaf worthy of display. But after about ten minutes of looking, something strange occurred.

All of a sudden, and to my surprise, the forest floor started popping with Crayola color; burnt orange, brick red, lemon yellow. The leaves seemed to be rising airily from the ground, as if I were wearing 3-D glasses. It was an extraordinarily arousing and educational experience. My old eyes suddenly became new again, as my brain adjusted to its new environment and child-like instructions.

The English biologist and politician John Lubbock wrote, "What we see depends mainly on what we look for." Where you are and what you attend to conditions what you see. If you look for beauty, ideas and meaning, you'll find it. If you look for data, statistics, and shortcomings, you'll find them.

If you start looking at marketplace ideas through a cultural lens, you'll soon find evidence of socially-influenced belief all around. They'll start popping out of the landscape as brightly and distinctly as those leaves on my path.

People are Other People

One of the most famous episodes of the TV series *The Twilight Zone* starred Burgess Meredith as Henry Bemis, a guy who loves books but who is surrounded by people who thwart his efforts to read them. The episode follows Bemis through the cataclysmic end of the world, revealing, among other thematic elements, that existence without other people is unbearable.

That episode always makes me ponder strange questions like: If there were no other people in the world, how often would I change my clothes? Would I shave? Which MP3 player would I use? Would I squeeze a lime into the neck of a beer bottle? I certainly wouldn't wear a yellow rubber wristband. What would I eat? What would I drink? What would I drive? What would drive *me*?

What drives me, you, and everyone else are our values, beliefs, and priorities, and those *ideas* come from other people. We do what we do largely because of the influence of those around us, through observation and direct interaction and from exposure to images and stories in the media. As the American philosopher Eric Hoffer said, "When people are free to do as they please, they usually imitate each other."

The world we've created is strange. It's real. It's all invented. And it's in a state of constant change. Why do we eat birds' eggs, fried strips of a pig, and grilled bread covered with an emulsion of fat globules for breakfast? Why do we pay to walk on circular conveyor belts and ride bicycles that go nowhere? Why do we do the wave at ballgames and pay handsomely for rubbery hotdogs and watery beer in plastic cups?

Recently, a seventh-grader in New York saved her choking friend's life using the Heimlich maneuver. She learned the technique from watching the optimistic cartoon character *SpongeBob SquarePants* use it to retrieve a clarinet lodged in Squidward's throat. Last year, the most popular baby names in the U.S. were Isabella and Jacob, the names of lead characters in the vampire-romance series, *Twilight*.

In the not too recent past, cocaine was a popular ingredient in teething remedies, allergy medications, and carbonated beverages (brain tonics); heroin was produced by Bayer and marketed as a cough suppressant in children's medicine (*heroic* help for coughs); and tattoos were the domain of prisoners and drunken sailors.

Are we all crazy?

Yes, we are. We're crazy for novelty *and* for meaning. We're crazy to stand out *and* to fit it. We're crazy for connection. We're crazy, social creatures. And when you finally realize this fact, the mysteries of the marketplace become clear.

Being social is *being one* with the crazies. It's about caring and listening. It's about sharing and participating. However, the *power* of social in creating belief in your idea lies in the connection you facilitate *between* people *around* your idea. Read it again: *You* must facilitate social engagement *through* your idea.

Every subculture has its peculiarities, but at the end of the day we're all made up of the same DNA. We all have the same social hungers. Social is about feeding those hungers.

It's about providing an encouraging environment, unique content, or an interesting experience that enables your audience to feel special because of their association with you, and to use that connection to bond with others.

Social is not the same thing as buzz. Buzz is social without a meaningful connection to a shared idea. Balloon Boy was buzz. The Segway was buzz. Evian's roller-skating babies were buzz. Buzz is about drawing attention. It's fleeting. It's about "it."

Social is about *giving* attention. Social provides people with common ground. It helps them connect, interact, and add meaning and value. It creates a shared experience and a sense of identity and belonging. It makes *your* idea part of the fabric of *their* social lives. It creates "we."

What Do You Mean by "We?"

One morning while standing in line at the local coffee shop, I overheard a group of guys talking about an upcoming professional basketball game. One of them, the smallest of the bunch, was passionately ranting about how *their* team should play that night (they were clearly fans) and he started every pronouncement with, "We . . ." *We* should do this. *We* shouldn't do that. *We* have to watch out for so and so and on and on.

Finally, one of his friends looked down at him, smirked, and in a smart-alecky Boston accent asked, "Who is this 'we' you keep referring to anyway?"

Social helps create that empowering feeling of *we*. It feeds people's hungers for acceptance and attention. It lets your audience think, "I'm not crazy. Look at the others like me." And that feeling brings them back, again and again.

The Web of Life

Don't resist the future. In one form or another, online social platforms and tools like Facebook, LinkedIn, and Twitter are here to stay. They're incredibly powerful means for like-minded people to interact, advance their agendas, and feed each other's social hungers.

But be wise and shape the tools, without letting the tools shape you. Participation in social networks is a time-sucking diversion without useful and interesting ideas that can be shared, enjoyed, and advanced. It's meaningless without content and conversations that connect people to each other and to what you do.

The same is true of real world environments, like cookouts, churches, clubs, and workplaces. Social provides those ideas. Social breathes life into shared experiences.

Social helps people associate with your values *and* connects them with others like them. It helps them signal identity and allegiance, start conversations and share experiences. It helps them mentally join a meaningful, albeit temporary community of like-minded people. It helps them feel alive.

Social does that by providing *currency* to your audience, currency *they* can use to feed *their* social hungers.

Social is an environment that you orchestrate and bring to life with new and interesting ideas where people can hang out, chat and contribute. It's an inviting, real world location like Starbucks. It's also an online community like Ravelry.com, where over 600,000 lovers of fiber arts come to socialize and share ideas.

Social is a cool or unusual product that people use to attract attention and interest. It's BMW's Mini Cooper. It's a TAG Heuer watch. It's a limited-edition, hand-painted pair of Vans sneakers. It's Seattle-based Jones Soda's flavored holiday concoctions.

Social gives people a *popular* way to start conversations, forge connections, and share their passions.

Social is also a meaningful story to share with others.

The Shirt off His Back

One Sunday, about ten years ago, I arrived late and checked into my room at a sleepy hotel in the middle of nowhere. I had an especially important presentation early the next morning, so my plan was to unpack, grab a bite to eat in the hotel restaurant and head off to bed.

As I unpacked my suit bag to deal with the inevitable wrinkles, I was shocked by my discovery: Suit? Check. Matching silk tie? Check. Belt? Check. Shoes? Check. Socks? Check. Dress shirt? . . . Dress shirt? . . . Shirt?! . . . Houston, we have a problem.

I glanced at my watch and realized that every store in the area, however few there must have been, had been closed for hours. Now what? I shook my head, rolled my eyes, closed the door to my room and headed down to the empty hotel bar.

After ordering a sandwich and making small talk with the bartender, the shirt catastrophe naturally came up. He agreed that my situation "sucked," and that, indeed, the stores were all closed and wouldn't reopen until well after my morning meeting was underway.

He then poured me a local beer, urged me to relax, and turned to serve two new customers who had just entered the area. I grabbed a pen and small notebook and started jotting down random thoughts (there were no smart phones or iPads back then).

After what seemed like a matter of minutes, I felt a tap on my shoulder. I turned to find my bartender holding up a hanger with something wrapped in dry cleaning plastic.

"Here you go. I'm pretty sure it will fit."

I blinked in disbelief at what I was seeing.

"You look about my size," he said. "So I called my girlfriend and had her grab one of my freshly pressed, white dress shirts for you."

Needless to say, I was blown away. And I reciprocated in a heartfelt and surprising way. But here's the strange thing: Whenever I need to tell a moving story about exceptional service, I don't tell that one. It lacks social currency. It's missing the identity-enhancing "we" that makes it valuable to share.

I felt no connection whatsoever to the hotel. There was nothing special about it, no shared association. So sharing *their* story would do nothing to feed *my* hungers for affiliation and identity.

Instead, I choose to use someone else's story; one I heard about another speaker and his experience at a Ritz-Carlton. Strangely, there's more *currency* for me in telling *his* story than in telling my own, because I get to trade on the celebrity status of the Ritz-Carlton brand. When I tell his story, the association oddly rubs off on me (I told you, we're all crazy).

Social turns the *audience* into the star by giving them status to use . . . *your* status. Ritz-Carlton strategically creates that kind of currency for its audience. Their people are trained to be on the lookout for ways to orchestrate unique experiences and create currency that's meaningful to its guests and built to spread. And their people are rewarded for creating those stories, with ever-increasing co-created value, pride of association, and internal attention and recognition.

Story creation and retelling at Ritz-Carlton has become a form of *employee* social currency that everyone shares, up and down the corporate hierarchy, on a daily basis. It keeps their people engaged, interested and passionately believing in the Ritz-Carlton idea.

It's not the words in the corporate credo that matter. It's the stories. It's the conversations between people that unlock Doors. As the old management saw goes, culture trumps strategy. Infuse your organization with spirit, excitement, and pride, stimulate talking and sharing, and your idea will expand in the same way that a spoonful of yogurt cultures a large pot of milk.

Can any Idea be Made Social?

Could the hotel in my shirt story employ a social component in the design of its idea? Of course. The issue is purely one of mindset.

Social isn't as simple as giving your audience a story to share or a proverbial t-shirt to wear. There has to be an emotional connection to the meaning behind the t-shirt, as well as to the aesthetics of the t-shirt, and, especially to the other people wearing the t-shirt.

Social is about the value of your idea, *and* your audience's ability and desire to use that value to feed their hungers.

The Marketplace of Ideas is Alive

The marketplace is an ever-shifting, always evolving social organization. Any idea can be turned into a protagonist for societal change and create feelings of shared passion. But to do so, you have to *elevate* your idea to something meaningful, something with soul. And then you have to energize it and bring it to life in a way that *stimulates* interaction and sharing, and which enhances the link between people's lives and your idea.

Unilever *elevated* Dove from a cleansing and moisturizing idea to a statement about beauty in an age of Photoshop and cosmetic surgery. Its *Campaign for Real Beauty* is about celebrating the natural beauty of all women and inspiring them to feel good about themselves. The company then *stimulated* conversations and fed people's social hungers with an incredibly powerful video called *Dove Evolution,* and with follow-on social catalysts in the form of online films, print advertisements, billboards, workshops, sleepover events, and even a book and a play.

So there's soap. Google did it with 1s and 0s. Red Bull did it with a foul-tasting beverage. Apple did it with an MP3 player. Nike did it with a sneaker. What's holding you back?

DOOR THREE SUMMARY

We want to be engaged. We want to be entertained. We want to get lost in an idea. But we don't want to "suspend disbelief," like we do while watching a movie. We *want* to believe. We ache to believe.

There's a growing hunger for meaning and truth in the world. People desperately want something they can believe in, and feel a part of, something bigger than themselves, an idea with purpose and soul.

The Key to unlocking the Door to Belief is to feed that hunger, to forget the language of logic and arguments and become proficient at the language of feelings and culture. Everything is subjective. Every decision is driven by what's inside someone, not what's on the outside.

Belief is a feeling. Vivid communication arouses those feelings. Tangible, heartfelt actions reinforce those feelings. Seeing an idea being used, worn and talked about confirms those feelings.

The Scottish philosopher David Hume wrote, "Belief is nothing but a more vivid, lively, forcible, firm, steady conception of an object, then what the imagination alone is ever able to maintain." It's also nothing less.

QUESTIONS TO ASK YOURSELF ABOUT
THE DOOR TO BELIEF

Are we being passionate and real? Is our communication and behavior an audacious statement about what we believe in and what life should be about for our audience?

Have we brought our idea to life in a vivid way? Is it visually powerful, clear and memorable?

Are we focused on their truth? Are we telling a meaningful and engaging story laced with details and emotion? Or are we focused on our facts, and trying to persuade people with carefully crafted arguments and mounds of data?

Do our actions *prove* what we believe in and care about? Do we demonstrate our uniqueness through small acts of caring and bold strokes of creation?

How can we make our idea easier or more desirable to talk about or share? How can we make it part of their social lives?

What *is* our meaningful idea? Why would people want to be a part of it and share it?

Bring Your Idea
to Life

Vision without action is a daydream.
Action without vision is a nightmare.

—Japanese proverb

Friday, January 12, 2007, 7:51 a.m. The start of Joshua Bell's 43-minute nightmare.

The idea: Bell, one of the world's greatest violinists, busks for change as an incognito street entertainer in a Washington D.C. Metro subway station.

The audience: 1,000-odd, rush-hour passersby.

The result: Seven people stopped to listen to Bell. He collected a grand total of $32.17 from 27 people, excluding $20 from the one person who recognized him, thus having her hunger for celebrity fed.

Despite being an internationally acclaimed virtuoso and performing moving masterpieces on one of the most valuable violins ever made, the Doors to Joshua Bell's audience remained tightly locked.

That case study, an awkward and at times painfully humbling experience for Bell, was initiated by the *Washington Post* as an experiment in "context, perception and priorities," and to assess whether beauty alone could unlock the Doors to Engagement, Interest, and Belief. Sadly, and despite the fact the Joshua Bell routinely enchants audiences worldwide with his breathtaking virtuosity, it could not.

There's your modern day marketplace parable: Preoccupied, stressed out people; an exceptional, refined idea; and, in affect *and* effect, nothing. Nada.

A brilliant and meaningful idea, even if placed directly in people's paths, is simply not enough to unlock the Doors to opportunity today. Please don't delude yourself into believing that it is. The results will break your heart and your spirit. Passion without understanding eventually burns out.

The artist Flora Whittemore wrote, "The doors we open and close each day decide the lives we live." The Doors we open in the marketplace determine the destiny of our ideas.

The Hidden Logic of Success

The Greek author Plutarch wrote, "What we achieve inwardly will change outer reality." Outer reality—the Doors to *other* people's guts, minds and hearts (their engagement, interest, and belief)—can *only* be unlocked by first unlocking the Doors to your own *inner* reality. Paradoxically, you have to come at *your* Doors in reverse order (belief, interest, engagement).

Your heart must lead the way. You must *believe* passionately in the integrity of your idea—in your mission to change things and make a difference—*before* you get your head and gut involved. Are you turned on by your idea? Do you love what you do? Do you love who you do it with and for? The most successful people and organizations achieve their success through a deeply held belief in their work. Their profits come from passion and purpose, not from setting and managing financial goals.

The *Washington Post* social experiment was a total head game. The people involved certainly believed that Bell's music, his idea, *could* bring happiness and meaning to people's lives. But they were indifferent as to whether or not it actually did. Their heart and soul simply weren't in it, and the results confirmed their purely academic approach and lack of caring.

Don't let the same thing happen to you and your idea. Establish and legitimize your other-focused idea with energy, supporting structures and processes, *then* turn on your mind and the powerful intellectual capacities of your people and creative partners. Turn your *interest* towards your audience, adding value to their lives and uniquely feeding *their* hungers. Remember, you're no longer competing for market share. You're after *heart share* and *mind share*.

Finally, for God's sake, have some imagination and guts. Stand for important, one-of-a-kind ideas in this world overflowing with me-too thinking. Try something new. Unlock the Doors to opportunity and separate your idea from the multitude of others.

Emerson declared, "To believe your own thought, to believe that what is true for you in your private heart, is true for all men, that is genius." Stop questioning yourself. Believe your own thought. Let your private heart lead the way for your head and gut.

Approach the world with openness and empathy, and boldly bring your idea to life. Feed people's hungers.

Google didn't invent search. Nike didn't invent running shoes or athletic gear. Starbucks didn't invent coffee or the coffee house. Amazon didn't invent online retailing. Harley didn't invent the motorcycle. Apple didn't invent the computer, the MP3 player, or the cell phone. They all brought common ideas to life in an engaging, desirable, and believable way. They fed their audiences hungers.

Start with your own Doors. Feed your own hungers. Have a compassionate heart and be inspired to change the world with your creativity and resourcefulness. Be bold and create something that is meaningfully different. Come alive and help others come alive.

A Tale of Two Artists

Vincent van Gogh and Pablo Picasso were two of the most influential artists of modern times; their paintings are now among the world's most popular and expensive works of art. Yet van Gogh died penniless, while Picasso's estate was valued at more than $750 million at the time of his death.

According to Professor Gregory Berns in his book *Iconoclast*, this disparity was due to Picasso's superior networking skills. He knew how to feed the hungers of influential people, who in turn helped enhance his name, reputation and bank account.

Both Picasso and van Gogh were extremely passionate about their work; they loved what they did. But Picasso was vibrant and alive. He understood how to unlock other's Doors and make *them* feel alive; van Gogh did not. Picasso knew how to make others happy; van Gogh was inwardly focused and struggled with relationships.

If you want people to seek you out and advance your idea, like Picasso in his time, remember that success in the marketplace is about adding value to the lives of others. It's about turning *them* on. It's about engaging *their* interests. It's about feeding *their* hungers. It's about making *them* happy. It's about bringing your idea to life for *their* benefit.

I wish this was not the case. I'd prefer the Doors didn't exist. I wish my ideas would be adopted on, what I believe to be, their merits alone. I want people to simply listen to me, buy my books, do what I recommend, tell their friends about me and what I do, feed *my* hungers. The world doesn't work that way.

They Just Don't Get It

I'm sure van Gogh, and others who have struggled to have their ideas appreciated and adopted, have voiced these familiar words, "They just don't get it." You've heard them. I've heard them hundreds of times over the years, and, on occasion, have caught myself expressing the same frustration.

We shouldn't misdirect *our* disillusionment and disappointment towards "them," our prospects, clients, constituents, bosses, co-workers, family members, et al. "They won't let me . . . *Life* won't let me . . ." simply means that we have not done what we need to do to unlock *their* Doors. If it's our idea, then it's about *us*. The responsibility for our passion is *ours* . . . and ours alone.

What do you want? Do you want a new job? Do you want a

promotion? Do you want your project funded? Do you want your method or cause adopted? Do you want people to embrace your idea, your art, you? Do you *really* want it? If you do, you'll pull out all the stops. You'll venture the adventure and bring others along on the journey with you. You'll inspire them to buy into your idea. You'll seduce them and get them excited to be a part of your idea. You'll get them to *feel* your idea through your creativity and passion. You'll make *your* idea *their* idea. You'll unlock their Doors.

Emerson declared, "Sometimes a scream is better than a thesis." Today's marketplace imperative lies not in writing a business plan nor in building a business model, although understanding why someone would engage with you as well as how you will feed and grow the idea over time is critical. Today's burning imperative is to create a pervading sense of passion, of determination to create something distinctive and compelling, to make a difference.

Get rid of your legacy and the life you've planned—the one that provides the illusion of safety and security—so you can embrace the life that's calling you. Don't dream your life away. Live your dream! Dare to value and take pleasure in the extremes. Let the pull of what turns you on, and what you care most deeply about, be your guide. Opportunity is screaming for you to stand out, to call upon those hidden reserves of compassion, competence, and guts and become the impassioned catalyst and architect for change that we all so desperately need.

Value Is Driven by Scarcity

Scarcity comes from distinction. And distinction comes from being bold and meaningfully different. Rediscover your unbridled imagination and idealistic hopes, and create new and preemptive benefits. Shatter what conventional wisdom tells you can be done. Pour your heart into your idea. And pour your soul into bringing it to life.

Erich Fromm wrote, "You have to stop in order to change direction." Stop and ask yourself, and your people: Are we asserting integrity of purpose in everything that we do? Does our desire to improve our customers' lives shine through in each and every action we take? Are our actions daring and inspiring? If not, change direction.

Now is not the time to "go along to get along." It's time to make waves, and then ride them. It's time to think very practically about how to uniquely add value to people's lives and pursue those ideas with daring. It's time to make history.

The most important thing you can leave the world, the most important thing you can leave your children, is not the results of your work. It's the tale of your journey. It's the fears overcome. It's the obstacles encountered. It's the lessons learned. It's to serve as an example and an inspiration.

Be an enemy of the ordinary, secure in the knowledge that the creatures of the commonplace will continue to sit passively and wait for things to change. Don't wait. Your business *is* ideas. Your ideas are you. They're your life. And your life is now.

Sign-off

*Whatever you can do, or dream you can do, begin it. Boldness
has genius, power, and magic in it. Begin it now.*
—Johann Wolfgang von Goethe

The marketplace is life, which makes it complex beyond
imagination. We'll never really know what we're capable of until
we try. And as in life, we are all prone to missteps and being
blindsided by the unexpected. To be wise means to concede to
our fallibility and to the unknown, and to keep learning and
moving forward with boldness, with integrity of purpose and
imaginative vision.

None of us is perfect. But we can carry a perfect idea in our
heart. We can live with passion and originality. It's the geniuses
who push forward with their unique ideas and personality who
transform the world and make history. Take Eleanor Roosevelt's
advice to heart, "Do one thing every day that scares you."
Become fully engaged and break out of the pack. Be bold and
bring your idea to life in a daring, creative way. Reject convention
in favor of an open, exciting and adventurous approach.
Godspeed. I hope this book helps.

About the Author

Tom Asacker is the author of three critically acclaimed books: *A Little Less Conversation* and *A Clear Eye for Branding*, groundbreaking books that redefine business for the new, customer-controlled economy, and *Sandbox Wisdom*, a heartwarming story about a CEO's search for meaning and success in the world of business and work. A popular speaker, Tom lectures to corporations, associations, and universities around the world, and works confidentially with executives and management teams at a number of world-class companies.

Prior to his role as a writer, professional speaker and corporate catalyst, Tom was an agitator in management posts at GE and throughout his entrepreneurial endeavors as founder of an internet startup; owner of an electronics manufacturing firm; and co-founder and CEO of a medical device company. He is a recipient of the George Land Innovator of the Year Award; he holds medical patents and product design awards; and he is recognized by Inc. Magazine, MIT, and YEO as a past member of their "Birthing of Giants" entrepreneurial executive leadership program. Tom holds a degree in Economics and Business Management, and lives in the great Northeast.

Visit www.opportunityscreams.com to learn more.